The Dawn of the Fossil Fuel Era

The Dawn of the Fossil Fuel Era

THE END OF "PEAK OIL"

—

Rex Tracy

ISBN-13: 9781523212576
ISBN-10: 1523212578
Library of Congress Control Number: 2016900276
CreateSpace Independent Publishing Platform
North Charleston, South Carolina

Front Cover Image Courtesy of iurii/Shutterstock
Rear Cover Image Courtesy of Nightman1965/Shutterstock

Table of Contents

Preface

————

As the manuscript was being finalized for this book at the beginning of 2016, the United States had just signed the Paris Agreement, in which some two hundred countries attending the COP21 summit of the UN Framework Convention on Climate Change agreed to limit atmospheric warming to 2 degrees (1.5 degrees if feasible) Celsius above preindustrial levels by 2080. This development quickly stoked headline opinion columns, such as one from CNN entitled "This Is the End of Fossil Fuels," by John Sutter. *Forbes Magazine Online* published "Paris Climate Change Deal Could Spell the Beginning of the End of the Fossil Fuel Age," written by Mike Scott. The thinking widely reported by the media is that such a cap on global mean temperature increases would effectively mean zero greenhouse-gas emissions between 2050 and 2080, and logically that would entail the effective end of fossil fuels as a primary source of energy worldwide.

This book is much more closely aligned with the sentiments expressed by Brad Plumer in a mid-December article he posted on Vox.com entitled "Have We Hit 'the End of the Fossil Fuel Era'? Not Even Close." Mr. Plumer soberingly points out that at the time the Paris Agreement was signed, fossil fuels comprised some 86 percent of the world's energy supply. This book will demonstrate that while this mix will migrate toward renewables over time, the hard fact is that fossil fuels will still be over 60 percent of the mix a quarter century from now. While limiting greenhouse gas and other emissions is a laudable goal, the reality is that the end of the fossil-fuel era has been predicted many times before and proven to be false. We are burning more fossil fuels now than ever before for one primary reason: the cost of alternative fuels is simply not competitive. As this book will make clear, the supply of fossil fuels is massive, and new discoveries are routinely being made. The extraction techniques have been perfected to the point where the abundance is cheaply harvested around the world. New technologies, such as hydraulic fracture and horizontal drilling, are unlocking previously unattainable supply and affordable costs. The advocates of alternative energy may well be right regarding the long-run share of coal as a primary fuel; now that natural gas has become so abundant and burns cleaner, coal will be hit "from all sides" and decline markedly as part of the energy mix. This book will focus on oil and gas because due to hydraulic fracture and horizontal drilling, both oil and gas are experiencing a pronounced resurgence in production that will likely continue until near midcentury.

Additionally, no one has ever really challenged the notion that we have abundant supplies of coal. (Ever heard anyone advocate that we are approaching "peak coal"?) Even though the demand for coal is expected to increase for the next quarter century, the future of coal over the long run is murky; for oil and gas, this is less so, given recent technological advancements. While wind and solar are viable over the long run, their competitiveness with existing fossil-fuel sources is decades away.

In the aftermath of the Paris Agreement, we again hear the siren song of renewables as savior. This is not the first time we have heard the heralding of a new energy era, and it will not be the last time we are told the fossil-fuel hegemony is coming to an end. Only a decade ago, there was a rash of books predicting the "end of oil" or "peak oil," where the production of crude oil would peak somewhere between 2015 and 2025 and subsequently either flatline and then steadily decline or descend into a rapid decline, taking the world economy down with it either way. Economic ruin in the short run was regularly predicted as skyrocketing crude prices destroyed disposable income, rendering the entire "suburban experiment" an economic train wreck. The purpose of this book is to reflect on the peak-oil intellectual movement and examine the track record of those who have regularly preached the end of carbon-based energy as we know it. Frankly, the predictive track record of the antihydrocarbon crowd is quite dismal, and for anyone thinking about where to park investment dollars, the question is rather simple for the near term. Is your money going to give you a better return being placed in the equity of a major energy company, such as ExxonMobil or Shell Oil, or is it better spent speculating on a start-up like Solyndra?

We are often told that the American suburban experiment is one of the largest misallocations of resources in human history. Yet one hundred years into it, the suburban development is still going strong. Petroleum is as cheap and inexpensive as ever, and the world is awash in crude oil, with robust known reserves. This is not to say that it is folly to pursue the alternative energy sources—we should, with all due haste. The point is that the transition from fossil fuels to wind and solar energy is likely to take much longer than advocates of alternative energy are willing to admit. When you undertake a more in-depth analysis, and looking at the hard unrelenting economics, oil and gas are going to have a massive cost advantage for most of the rest of the century. This book is an exercise in exploring why.

An additional theme discussed repeatedly throughout this book is the notion of constant ingenuity. For example, hydraulic-fracture techniques were first experimented with in 1947, with the first commercially viable drilling occurring using the technique in 1950; yet it would be another half century before the full effects of these methods would be realized. As recently as 2006, there were very few predicting the massive upsurge in crude-oil production in the United States' "tight" or "unconventional" formations, such as shale and shale rock, and there was an entire chorus telling us at the time that crude production either had peaked, was peaking, or would peak shortly. Here we are in 2016, with the largest abundance of crude oil in history, with known reserves keeping pace. The point is that no one knows for certain when we will reach the end of oil or when production will peak. Assuming it is in the near term downplays the role of technological innovation, which frankly has a much better track record for performance than do the predictors of gloom, who have made erroneous prognostications about the long-run viability and availability of petroleum for most of my adult life.

The reason for writing a book on the matter is that there is much at stake in getting the policy right. Many of the advocates for alternative energy have routinely espoused artificial measures to bring the cost of petroleum-based fuels into line with alternative sources. Whenever you hear someone advocating large increases in gasoline taxes for environmental protection or the reduction of greenhouse gases, you encounter such an argument. A carbon tax would do likewise. In the early 1990s, the Clinton administration formally proposed a tax based on British thermal units, or the BTU tax. This, too, would have acted to neutralize the low-cost advantage fossil fuels have over yet-to-be-perfected alternative energy sources. A carbon or outright gasoline tax would indeed close the cost advantage enjoyed by fossil-fuel-based distillates, but the economic damage of doing so is far reaching. While the affluent environmental-lawyer lobbyist in Washington, DC, working on K Street, can afford such cost increases in everyday living, wide swaths of the middle- and working-class citizens cannot. The environmental left is quick to bemoan the stagnant middle-class wages over the past forty years but then is equally quick on the draw in advocating very regressive energy-related taxes in the effort to reduce carbon emissions.

Please understand that no matter what carbon-reduction initiatives the United States undertakes, the vast increase in carbon emissions from China and India more than offset such efforts from a net basis. Are China and India really going to consign hundreds of millions of their citizens to the poverty that accompanies low carbon consumption? Can China afford to do so when vast swaths of its society do not share in the prosperity of the coastal regions and seethingly resent it? What does China's internal stability look like without growth driven by energy consumption where the have-nots are still measured in the hundreds of millions? Are wind and solar energy really ready to power whole economies? If so, why have they not done so already? While wind and solar power are growing at a double-digit pace annually, that is from a minuscule base and will take many decades to catch up to and exceed the carbon-based sources. Even that assumes a static technological base for fossil fuels. As we have seen over the last decade, the oil and gas industry is capable of very potent technological developments, making the economical extraction of previously difficult to attain deposits quite feasible.

Furthermore, the gap between the cost of generating a BTU from an alternative energy source, such as wind and solar, versus that of oil and gas is getting even larger as these words are written due to the collapse of crude prices during 2014–2015. Had the cost of crude stayed at say $125 per barrel, then the incentive to migrate to cars powered by electricity generated from a wind- or solar-sourced power plant would have been more realistic.

And then there is the problem of battery storage. We need to bear in mind that battery technology simply is not at a place where driving an electric car is feasible—no matter the cost of fuel. Do you really want to try a road trip in an electric car and hope you can find the electrical outlets you will need along the way? Care to try that on a summer day in the Utah or California desert? Even just driving to and from work poses logistical challenges—though admittedly those are becoming more manageable for electrically powered cars with each passing year. The point is that while steady progress in alternative sources for energy is methodically proceeding apace, parity with our fossil-fuel-driven transportation infrastructure is decades upon decades away. And that does not even touch on the high price of electric cars. While a Hollywood mogul or rich executive can entertain their alternative-fuel hobbies and proclivities, the average commuter coming to work from the suburbs or exurbs cannot. A $100,000 Tesla is not really a viable option for the average American family, and neither is the Chevrolet Volt or the myriad of other electric-car options. While massive strides have been made in the area of eclectic-vehicle technology over the years, much more needs to be done to make them commercially viable for mass consumption.

The cold reality, as this book will demonstrate, is that contrary to everything we were led to believe would be the case by now, fossil fuels exist in abundance and are affordable, and they are likely to remain so long into the future. There is no doubt that alternative sources of fuel will one day reign supreme, but that day is far off in the future. There is little doubt that at some point, we will reach the moment when the production of crude oil reaches its peak—someday. Should economic and social policy be based on hard facts and economic fundamentals or the oil-scarcity guessing game? As for the reduction of carbon emissions, the switch from coal to natural gas offers by far the best short-term hope for reducing carbon emissions. This book will not spend a great deal of time on the issue of climate change, for the thrust of the book is primarily to refute the notion that we are nearing the point where we have reached peak-oil production. Frankly, this author would be willing to engage more in the climate-change debate if the advocates were more serious in their arguments. There is no reason to automatically dismiss nuclear energy as a carbon-free source of energy capable of generating massive amounts of BTUs in the decades and centuries to come, but the global-climate advocates refuse to even entertain a discussion on the use of nuclear power. For that constituency, it really is about the preoccupation with renewable energy in the short term despite all the facts suggesting this is many decades in the making. The position this book takes is that the world economy will, in fact, migrate to carbon-free energy sources over time—a whole lot of time—and that fossil fuels carry the day in the interim. Peak oil will have to wait, and the ingenuity of the oil industry will ensure that it does.

It is also worth considering that, as a consequence of abundant and affordable hydrocarbons, the barrier for alternative fuels is high economically because it will be next to impossible, as the struggling American middle class, to arbitrarily pay more for basic daily energy needs in the face of existing economic fuel sources. Arguably the only real way to get a mass migration to electric cars and alternative energy at this point would be with the use of coercive government policy via tax policy. Left up to purely market forces, fossil fuels win in the near and intermediate term hands down and could wind up being more competitive long term than anyone realizes at this point in time.

Regular readers of energy literature will also note that this book does not spend any time on either the geopolitical history or US history surrounding crude oil or natural gas (other than to touch on the history of hydraulic fracturing as a drilling method). This work is focused on squaring off against the notion that we are running out or somehow nearing peak production. A full accounting of the history of oil has already been more than adequately done by Daniel Yergin in his seminal work *The Prize*. William Manchester's *The Glory and the Dream* is another fine historical account of the major developments of the mid-twentieth century and touches on some of the major events concerning energy history occurring during that time. Morgan Downey's *Oil 101* and Russell Gold's *The Boom: How Fracking Ignited the American Energy Revolution and Changed the World* are also detailed accounts of the history of hydraulic fracture as an extraction technique and its impact on world-energy markets. For readers who are interested in reading the role of oil in connection with nineteenth-, twentieth-, and early twenty-first-century history, these works are surely the place to start.

The fact that there is so much existing literature on energy and oil begs the question as to why write a book on the issue of oil abundance at all. The answer is that I have not found anything that challenges head on the many books written a decade ago that predicted peak oil and the doom that would follow. I do not take the position that discrediting peak oil is an exercise in self-evidence. I believe that as soon as crude prices spike again in a sustained way, there will be another rush of works predicting the end of oil, the decline of the West, and all the usual rot that goes with it. Thus, the aim of this book is to attack and debunk the notion of peak oil, since it has not, to this day, a century and half after the first oil wells were discovered, been successfully established as a credible theory. We keep finding more; technology keeps improving and allowing us to get at what we could not before. Peak-oil theory cannot tell us, with any degree of accuracy, when production will peak. Peak-oil proponents keep trying and keep failing because they need near-perfect information to make such predictions—which they do not have. There is no way they can know for certain, or even roughly, when our technological innovation will have maxed out the feasibility of extracting crude oil.[1]

One final comment regarding my background before getting on with the book: for those who find it salient, I am not affiliated with the oil and gas industry in any way. To my knowledge, I do not directly own nor have I ever directly owned shares of oil and gas companies or any other kind of energy company. There may be the possibility that fund managers for the 401(k) plans and IRAs I own have traded in such shares, but I have not directed the purchase of shares or corporate bonds of any individual companies, much less

---

1 For a comprehensive discussion on why the peak oil theory has failed over the decades to predict the exact point at which we will have reached the peak production of crude oil, see Alhadal A. Hussein, "Analysis: Why Hubbert's Peak Oil Theory Fails." *http://oilpro.com/post/18246/why-hubbert-peak-oil-theory-fails*, Posted September 7, 2015.

energy companies. I have no vested financial interest in taking any position that is bullish on the prospect of crude-oil distillates as an energy source for the decades to come. I have spent the better part of the past twenty-six years either studying law or performing law-related work for the financial-services industry in business areas that had nothing to do with the energy sector, much less petroleum companies. I am not a shill for the oil and gas industry, although I will freely admit that I find their tenacity, ingenuity, and resilience inspiring. I find it quite amazing that so many of my fellow Americans hold that industry in such contempt, given the wildly successful benefits we all receive from the abundance of cheap energy. We were all supposed to be facing economic calamity by now, and we are not—a fact largely owed to the stellar performance of the energy industry right here in America.

It is quite unfortunate that it will apparently take some kind of crisis for the average American to, once again, appreciate the low-priced fuel we now enjoy as well as the high quality of life it enables. It is often said that one never fully appreciates what he or she has until it's gone. Touché. To that extent, the energy industry—oil and gas providers in particular—is a victim of its own success. It has been so enormously successful in recent years that it appears we can take it for granted, the result of which is that the industry does not get the appreciation it deserves. Be that as it may, the success is likely to roll on for much time to come—with plenty of time to transition to alternative sources of fuel in an orderly way, without the catastrophe the "peak oilers" have been predicting for decades.

Introduction

————

THOSE OF US WHO GREW up as young children and early teen-agers in the 1970s vividly remember the gas shortages of 1973 and 1979 as we watched our parents scramble to beat gas-line rushes or worry about whether they could afford heating oil in the dead of winter. We recall the whole decade as one endless energy crisis, where price spikes were common-place enough that our parents seemed to speak in terms of a new paradigm of permanent shortage for many key energy sources. Discussion of energy efficiency, conservation, and dependence on foreign supplies was something I heard each and every year from the second grade through my high-school graduation in 1984. To be sure, these energy crunches certainly did not ruin my childhood; indeed, I look back on those years with the usual fondness one does regarding their early youth.

I will say, however, that I felt the angst caused by the sight of my parents getting up extra early to beat the gas lines and the dinner-table discussions about how to budget for ever-increasing fuel costs. I would speak about it with my dad when I became old enough to work, and we lamented that we didn't want to give up our lifestyle—that if we needed to work harder to earn more to pay for higher gas prices, then that was the price we were prepared to endure. You couldn't get through that decade without feeling the effects of high-energy costs in your bones—no matter what your age.

Those of us coming of age in that decade recall then president Carter excoriating what he referred to as profligate and wasteful energy-consumption habits. Americans were told by what seemed to be a nearly universal gauntlet of journalists, politicians, and academics to prepare for a future with lower energy use. It was said we would have to get by with less, contend with steadily increasing prices for energy to heat our homes and commutes to work, and to prepare for a new age of scarcity. The whole notion of free-market, free-enterprise capitalism was coming into question by some Ivy League scholars who published on the matter.[2]

In fact, the whole notion of limits to growth, which asserted energy scarcity and raw-materials shortages by the end of the millennium, would accompany would become a virtual cottage industry in those years. It is likely that the genesis for this intellectual movement was the publication of *Limits to Growth*,

---

2 See Rufus E. Miles Jr., *Awakening from the American Dream: The Social and Political Limits to Growth* (Universe Books, 1976). Mr. Miles was a cabinet member and advisor to three US presidents (Eisenhower, Kennedy, and LBJ.). According to the April 15, 1996, *New York Times* obituary on Mr. Miles, this book was a runner-up to a National Book Award in 1977. At the time he published this book, he was a senior fellow at the Woodrow Wilson School of Public and International affairs at Princeton University.

by Donella Meadows, Jorgen Randers, Dennis L. Meadows, and William W. Behrens III.[3] Other publications would follow over the next decade. Numerous academic research papers would assert and reassert the theme that exponential economic growth pitted against finite material resources, including energy, would necessarily lead to shortages until well into the Reagan presidency. Even today the limits-to-growth school of thought is alive and well. A quick search on the topic will yield a substantial number of articles and other writings looking back over the last forty years since the initial publication of the groundbreaking *Limits to Growth.*

The ultimate apex for the limits-to-growth perspective had to be *The Global 2000 Report to the President—Entering the 21st Century,* (the "Report") issued in 1980 and reissued in 1988 by hundreds of top scientists in the United States. The basic premise of the report was classic limits-to-growth theory—due to the finite nature of natural resources, we would eventually run out of oil, natural gas, arable land/farmland, and other natural-resource materials necessary for modern life.[4] The report clearly sided with the peak-oil line of thinking in the "Principal Findings" section, which stated, "During the 1990s world oil production will approach geological estimates of maximum production capacity, even with

---

3 Meadows, Randers, Behrens, and Meadows, *Limits to Growth* (Universe, 1972). Over the years, this work would sell over twelve million copies worldwide. It is unquestionably one of the single most successful writings on environmental issues ever published.

4 Gerald O. Barney, ed., *The Global 2000 Report to the President—Entering the 21st Century* (Dexter, MI: Thompson-Shore, Inc., 1980, 1988).

rapidly increasing petroleum prices."[5] The Report goes on page after page, asserting Malthusian predictions of depravity that essentially amounted to such hysterical doomsday pandering that would make Thomas Malthus proud.

As a youngster and teenager in the midst of all this Chicken-Little shrieking that the sky was falling, it was hard not to feel a deep-seated uneasiness about what lie ahead. What kind of world would I inherit as an adult? Were we, in fact, running out of everything? Would we actually have to live without basic commodities and other resources when I reached adulthood? Would my generation be bequeathed the same kind of America that our parents had? What would our everyday lives look like if we had less and less of the things we needed? Would our lives be restricted to large communal dwellings similar to housing projects, and would we have to rely solely on public transportation for physical mobility? Would the automobile return to being merely a toy for the super affluent? Indeed, for those early adolescent youngsters of that era who were naturally inclined to observe things around them, these questions were commonplace nearly the whole time we grew up. I vividly recall having a discussion with my grandfather in my early teens, somewhere around 1977–1978, where I reiterated a lesson in school I'd had earlier that year in which we were told that at current consumption rates, the world would run out of oil in about forty years.

Well, it is now 2016. Nearly forty years has come and gone, and the United States, along with the rest of the world,

---

5 Ibid., 2.

is awash in oil. Commodities of all types are in abundant supply, with their prices at multiyear lows. As a matter of fact, the proven oil reserves in the United States for 1977–1978 were 31.8 billion barrels of crude oil and lease condensate. Fast-forward to the twenty-first century, and that reserve number stood at 25.2 billion barrels as of 2010.[6] That number has continued to increase to 26.5 billion barrels in 2011.[7] Even more important, the trend is on a steep upward slope. In 2008, the EIA data had the US crude-oil reserves pegged at 19.1 billion barrels, so the increase to 2011 levels is 38.7 percent increase from the reserve lows of 2008. As this book will show in chapter 6, the US-proved reserves have continued to grow and, as of 2014,[8] reached a whopping 40 billion barrels—twice what it was during the financial crisis nearly eight years ago. You heard that correctly: US-proved crude-oil reserves have *doubled* in less than ten years.

The recent surge in American crude-oil production is a massively important development from a geopolitical, economic, and social perspective. Our standard of living depends on an abundant and inexpensive energy source, not just for the purpose of heating our homes or getting to and from work, but from the perspective of economic development and the growth of incomes and employment. I recall a colleague once telling me that the whole notion of suburban and

6 US Energy Information Administration, *Annual Energy Review 2011*, Table 4.2 (September 2012).

7 Ibid.

8 Proved Reserves as of YE 2014 is the latest data available by the US Energy Information Agency.

exurban living arrangements amounted to the most colossal misallocation or resources in the history of mankind. And frankly I had heard that line of thinking on and off for the better part of my entire life.

For much of the late twentieth century and today, there is an intellectual movement that seeks to discredit life outside the urban core—to dismiss it as unsustainable "sprawl" [9] and to bemoan the perceived "supposed entitlements of suburbia" and chalk up the entire suburban lifestyle as a project representing a set of tragic choices because it is a living arrangement with no future.[10] Over the years, I have often read pro-urban advocates repeatedly resort to growth choking, meaning to curb the incentives to live outside the formal city limits. Typical methods asserted to further suburban living include the elimination of the home-mortgage-interest tax deduction, which would gut the primary economic incentive to own a home versus rent an apartment, and a massive increase in the use of toll roads. Gasoline taxes are another means by which to add expense to suburban and exurban living.

But if the angst about sprawl is based, at least in part, on the notion that the world doesn't have the resources,

---

9 Perhaps the most audacious attacks on the suburban living arrangement come from the very outspoken pro-urban writer James Howard Kunstler, whose book *The Long Emergency: Surviving the Converging Catastrophes of the Twentieth Century*, clearly draws the nexus between peak oil and the end of the suburban lifestyle. The Atlantic Monthly Press published the book in 2005. Mr. Kunstler's positions on peak oil theory, his predictions, and his base attacks on suburbia will be discussed in further detail in chapter 2.

10 James Howard Kunstler, making the observation in a speech delivered at the meeting of the Second Vermont Republic on October 28, 2005.

especially petroleum, to support such a lifestyle, shouldn't we have seen this line of thinking result in its logical conclusion by now—forty years after the first Arab oil embargo? If suburban life, or life in the context of the free-enterprise system more generally, is not sustainable due to the finite nature of the resources that form the basis for modern industrial life, then shouldn't we have seen much more acute resource shortages than we have?

To be sure, in 2008, when the price of oil briefly touched $147 a barrel for West Texas Intermediate Crude, and US reserves reached the lowest point ever at nineteen billion barrels, the antigrowth movement seemed to be on the verge of a major historical inflection point where their intellectual premise looked to be vindicated beyond dispute. But then came the era when technologies like hydraulic fracture and horizontal drilling were perfected, the result of which has been a gusher of new production and a sharp increase in the proved US oil reserves. Both of these developments show little sign of abating over the long run, and we now regularly hear that the United States is expected to outproduce Saudi Arabia in crude-oil production later this decade. While US production supremacy worldwide is not expected to last longer than five to seven years, that the United States could even potentially lead the world in the production of crude oil at all would have been simply unthinkable a decade ago, yet here we are.

This stunning turn of events in recent years has not dissuaded the antigrowth left or those skeptical of free-enterprise principles from continuing with the assertion that we will peak in our ability to produce many key fossil fuels in the first half of this century. A 2014 article by Gail Tverberg posted on ourfiniteworld.com illustrates the persistence of the limits-to-growth line of thinking.[11] Tverberg charges with a frontal assault on the notion of oil abundance with a section of the article entitled "Individual citizens are easily misled by news stories claiming an abundance of oil."[12] She dismisses current oil supplies as nothing more than an outgrowth of the historically high price for oil, the large-scale availability of debt, and low interest rates.[13] Indeed, her pessimism is most assertive when she states as follows with respect to the limits-to-growth philosophy:

> How long can economic growth continue in a finite world? This is the question the 1972 book *The Limits to Growth* by Donella Meadows and others sought to answer. The computer models that the team of researchers produced strongly suggested that the world economy would collapse sometime in the first half of the 21st century.

---

11 "Limits to Growth at our Doorstep, but not Recognized," Tverberg, February 6, 2014, ourfiniteworld.com

12 Ibid.

13 Ibid. A counterpoint to this assertion will be argued later in this book to the effect that while high crude prices most certainly spur production increases as previously noneconomic sources become commercially viable with the higher price, this is not the only dynamic at play. The industry is getting massively more efficient with each passing year—motivated in large part to collapsing crude prices of 2014–2016.

I have been researching what the real situation is with respect to resource limits since 2005. *The conclusion I am reaching is that the team of 1972 researchers were indeed correct. In fact, the promised collapse is practically right around the corner, beginning in the next year or two.* In fact, many aspects of the collapse appear already to be taking place, such as the 2008–2009 Great Recession and the collapse of the economies of smaller countries such as Greece and Spain. How could collapse be so close, with virtually no warning to the population? (emphasis added).[14]

This was posted in February 2014, exactly two years ago as of the writing of this book, and the imminent "collapse" is nowhere in sight. As this book will show, natural-resource abundance is widespread; in fact, the commodities business is facing a once-in-a-lifetime level glut. There cannot be a glut when a resource is in oversupply. You cannot have scarcity and abundance at the same time. Arguments can be made that developed economies will struggle with economic growth and that their economies could collapse for any number of reasons. This book does not contend that there is an end to the business cycle. There will be recessions and depressions to come. What is being asserted is that over the long run, developed economies are not going to collapse because they have run out of oil or other fossil fuels. There is room for economic mismanagement to do all kinds of damage, but

---

14 Ibid.

in my view, that is a completely separate issue from whether natural resources are or are not in abundance.

The lack of any real evidence to support the notion of resource scarcity as a cause for limits to growth is exactly the purpose for undertaking the effort to write this book. This kind of thinking is so off the mark yet so commonplace among many of our purported intellectual elite that these unsupportable notions need to be publicly challenged. The environmental elite have a policy chokehold on the Obama administration to the point that it won't even approve the portion of the Keystone Pipeline project that would allow crude oil to flow freely from the Canadian oil sands in Alberta to the lower forty-eight US states. This is, no doubt, one of the biggest economic and energy policy "no-brainers" in modern economic history, yet year after year, we debate the merits of something that has the overwhelming support of the American people. Former secretary of state Hillary Clinton, a leading candidate for the 2016 Democratic Party nomination for president, has recently flipped her position to now oppose the pipeline—a clear sop to the environmental lobby.

I intentionally challenge the whole notion of limits to growth as an intellectual movement. This is a movement that, for decades, has preached that the world is running out of the things we need in a modern industrial age, but our ingenuity as a society and as a people leads to the procurement of ever-increasing amounts of various commodities—including petroleum. With the United States as a prime example, its economy grew several times over between 1970 and 2006, has continued to grow since, maintaining relatively steady oil reserves, and then saw a rapid expansion of those reserves since 2009. We are now in a position where we have a gusher of previously heretofore unplanned domestic crude supply. Furthermore we are now emerging from a commodities supercycle of the past fifteen years, with commodity prices materially slipping from their cyclical highs, notwithstanding that we have ever-increasing economic output. Prices for key commodities are well off their recent highs, while the world economy continues to chug along. And there's that pesky little fact that all the while we were in the last commodity supercycle, with its acute price increases from 2000 through 2008, the US economy grew.

Consider this book a polemic that argues vigorously that human ingenuity will facilitate the full development of all known oil supplies, whether they are merely technically recoverable but not a proved reserve in some accounting sense or an actual proved reserve worthy of reporting as such in a securities-and-exchange filing. The only question is at what price? Unlike Ms. Tverberg, I do not see higher oil prices as an inhibitor to their long-run extractability but rather the impetus for it. The higher the price a barrel of oil fetches on the open market, the more economic incentive there is to retrieve what we've known has been there for decades. As far as there being economic limits to what consumers will be able to afford, I will remind the reader that comparatively high prices of gasoline on a per-gallon basis in the early 1980s did not preclude what would become the longest peacetime economic expansion to date from occurring (some ninety-six months). Median family income rose smartly in that decade, and the high cost of gasoline in 1982–1983 was simply not a long-run impediment. In fact, what followed the sky-high prices of the early 1980s was a supply glut that devastated the US "oil patch" economically.

The book starts with chapter 1 discussing the absurdity of the notion that we are running out of oil. I will address the notion of peak oil and the predictions made by those who espouse it, and categorically dispute each and every claim with widely available data from public and governmental sources. This book will assert that we will not run out of oil in your lifetime. Even though its price may be volatile, it will be affordable. It may be more expensive than you'd like at times, but it won't even cost you as much as it did my parents in the 1970s as a percentage of their disposable income.

Chapter 2 will survey five large, publicly traded petroleum companies in terms of their outlook for oil production and consumption over the next thirty to forty years as well as their assessment of the state of fossil fuels generally. If we really are on the cusp of reaching peak oil, shouldn't we be seeing that fact reflected in their stock prices? Why is ExxonMobil among the most valuable companies on the face of the earth in terms of market capitalization (indeed of outstanding shares multiplied by the current stock price) if its core business is predicated on extracting and producing a commodity we are about to run out of? ExxonMobil has a $300-billion-plus market value, which is among the world's highest for any company regardless of industry affiliation. If, in fact, we are on the downward slope of what has been referred to as "Hubbert's Peak"[15]—the point at which world production peaks and is followed by a steady decline over time—shouldn't ExxonMobil be in a much more precarious position? If the oil companies are truly about to exhaust their reserves anytime in the foreseeable future, shouldn't that be reflected in the price of oil? Shouldn't we be seeing oil at much higher prices if it really is about to run out? Moreover, one can argue that the recent decline in stock prices for major oil companies and other petroleum-industry participants has to do with collapsing crude prices that began in the latter half of 2014 and accelerated throughout 2015. If anything, the industry is a victim of its own success. It has generated so much additional supply that the current glut of crude inventories act to depress profits for the industry. There is so much oil, and, as with any commodity, when there is abundance, the price goes down. This is Economics 101, and there is reason to believe the glut will continue for several more years.

Chapter 3 will explore the sustainability of new technologies. Hydraulic fracture ("fracking") has its origins dating back to the late 1940s.[16] Horizontal drilling is relatively new. Both

---

15 The term "Hubbert's Peak" is derived from the famous Shell Oil geologist Marion King Hubbert, who worked in the Shell research lab in Houston, Texas—he worked for Shell Oil from 1946 to 1964. The details of Hubbert's Peak theory will be discussed at length in chapter two.

16 American Petroleum Institute (API), *Hydraulic Fracturing—Primer, Unlocking America's Natural Gas Resources* (January 2014), 2. The API states as follows:

> Hydraulic fracturing has been used in the oil and natural gas industry since the 1940s, producing more than 600 trillion cubic feet of natural gas and 7 billion barrels of oil. Used with modern

are transforming the US production outlook[17] and causing a massive geopolitical readjustment, where the relative power of the OPEC cartel is being seriously undermined.[18] Is this a one- or two-decade phenomenon or is this something more durable, with impacts that will last half a century or more?

Chapter 4 will examine the recent developments in the area of methane clathrate, where a large amount of methane is trapped within a crystal structure of water that is similar to ice. These "gas hydrates," as they are often called, are found in vast quantities on the ocean floor in various deposit formations around the world. The vast availability of this carbon-based fuel opens the door to the prospect of methane possibly replacing natural gas as a primary source of energy in developed economies at some point in the future. Think of it as

---

horizontal drilling technology, fracking has unlocked vast US shale reserves, launching a renaissance in oil and natural gas production, creating tens of thousands of jobs and generating economic growth. Without these advanced technologies, we would lose 45 percent of domestic natural gas production and 17 percent of our oil production within five years." Ibid.

17 Ibid.

18 Ibid., 3. The API Report depicts an Energy Information Agency (EIA) chart that shows sharp increases in US crude-oil production since 2007, and a steep drop in US Crude Net Imports since then. The United States produced nearly eight billion barrels of crude in 2013, the highest level in decades. The current run rate for 2015 US crude production is on target to exceed nine billion barrels. The collapse in the price of crude in world markets will most certainly result in a pullback from these levels temporarily, but keep in mind that as recently as 2006, the United States was producing less than six million barrels. A decade later, the United States has increased that by 50 percent and is approaching the all-time US production record set in 1970.

sort of an energy bank, if you will. We are paying our energy bills with some old, established accounts (oil and natural gas), and it now appears those accounts are a little more flush with resources that should be open to development in the future.

Additionally this chapter will look at the potential feasibility of an automobile running on methane or natural gas in large commercial volumes and how that could prolong the current technically recoverable oil reserves. There is no question that a motor vehicle is capable of running on natural gas; I see metro buses running on it every day. The question is at what pace can the United States and world automotive and truck fleets shift over to natural gas as a primary fuel and what will be the impact on the cost of transportation (How many natural gas filling stations have you seen in your travels lately?)?

Chapter 5 will explore the supposition that if the technocrats were wrong on the available qualities of crude oil for use by mankind in the industrial age, isn't it likely they are also wrong about the inherent scarcity of other vital commodities necessary for modern life? The endless prognostications by the prophets of doom that we are running out of resources to continue the industrial age have been wrong for the better part of the past fifty years. Doesn't the recent reversal of fortune with crude oil and natural gas warrant a continued defense of the notion that human ingenuity coupled with the entrepreneurial spirit will lead to continuing abundance of the things we need to facilitate modern life? Do we really need to start watching the survival channel for ideas on what to do when "the end" arises? This chapter will cover several historical examples of human triumph, where the potential of scarcity has resulted either in well-executed substitution (switching one raw material with another to avoid the scarcity) or where a material that was thought to be on the verge of exhaustion underwent a rebirth from a reserve and production standpoint. The overriding theme of this chapter is that "necessity is the mother of invention," to quote an age-old adage.

Chapter 6 will explore some of the available evidence addressing the near-term future of fossil fuels—focusing, as this book does, on oil and gas. The threshold question for this chapter is what is the prospect for carbon-based energy (oil and gas)? Do we really face an era of scarcity not seen for a century and a half, or are we on the cusp of a new energy age of abundance—carbon abundance. Perhaps we muddle along with the "somewhere in between." This book will take the position and vigorously defend the notion that we are indeed at the outset of a new energy age. For at least another fifty years, that energy age will continue to be carbon based. Moreover, this chapter will assert that energy abundance will continue to result in comparatively cheap energy, meaning that any increase in petroleum or natural-gas retail prices will basically be in tandem with income growth over the long run. This cheap energy will be the catalyst for continued rapid economic growth and the development of technologies that make natural resource extraction sustainable over the long haul—at least the remainder of this century (that means the rest of your life and the life of your children).

It seems that in every period of economic stress, like the 2008 recession and its slow-growth aftermath, we hear from the agents of disaster. We are told we will need to radically alter our lives, that our personal consumption is the root of our problems, and that consumption is disease. This book will make the case that this kind of thinking is old and tired. We have many economic problems in urgent need of attention. When the vast majority of the income gains have gone to the richest 1 percent over the past forty years, with middle class living standards going nowhere over that period, we know we have a front-and-center economic issue. Resource scarcity simply has not proven to be a contributor to that long-term problem, as the limits-to-growth crowd predicted over the past several decades.

CHAPTER 1

Weren't We Supposed to Be Out of Oil by Now?

———

What are they thinking? They're thinking that it's [oil] running out, it's running out and 90 percent of what's left is in the Middle East. Look at the progression, Versailles, Suez, 1973, Gulf War 1, Gulf War 2. This is a fight to the death. So what are they thinking? Great! They're thinking keep playing, keep buying yourself new toys, keep spending $50,000 a night on your hotel room, but don't invest in your infrastructure...don't build a real economy. So that when you finally wake up, they will have sucked you dry, and you will have squandered the greatest natural resource in history..."

— Bryan Woodman, played by Matt Damon, in the 2005 movie *Syriana*

Peak Hysteria

THE FIRST TIME I'D EVER heard the term "peak oil" was sometime around the year 2000. I recall reading about Marion King Hubbert in a business publication on the topic of a recent spike in the price of oil, which had risen threefold from about ten dollars per barrel to just over thirty dollars in the period between 1998 to the latter part of 1999. To be sure, the notion of crude-oil scarcity and the inevitability of running out of this finite resource was a notion I had grown up with since before I was even ten years old. What seemed different this time was that I was now in my midthirties and feeling like all those warnings over the years meant that we were now living on borrowed time—the day of economic reckoning was indeed around the corner, and what remained might well be a new age where oil prices would rise inexorably into the future. In earlier periods when prices would spike, like the early 1980s and the early 1990s during the first Gulf War, I made every effort to remain agnostic and dispassionate and always felt vindicated for doing so when prices would eventually return to levels that existed before their spike.

This time seemed different. There was no crisis per se, at least not one of the magnitude that one could attribute to the tripling of the price per barrel in an eighteen-month period. OPEC had made a series of production cuts, apparently designed to increase the price per barrel, and did so with apparent great success. But there was no major war or great power confrontation that could be ascribed to this—just basic economic fundamentals of supply and demand. That OPEC countries had the power to control the price of crude oil, like they were turning a spigot handle, made it all the more plausible to ascribe to the scarcity notion—that it is basically running out and most of what is left is in the firm control of OPEC countries, and that would affect my life personally and profoundly.

As the decade wore on, the discussion of the end of oil would increase in both frequency and tone, becoming near hysteria by 2004–2005, with three books being published in that era, predicting doom economically and geopolitically. In 2004, *The End of Oil: On the Edge of a Perilous New World* was written by Paul Roberts, a contributor to *Harper's Magazine*, followed a year later by *The Empty Tank: Oil, Gas, Hot Air, and the Coming Global Financial Catastrophe*, written by Jeremy Leggett, a former faculty member of the Royal School of Mines in London in 2005.[19] Finally the *Long Emergency*, already referred to in the introduction to this book and written by James Howard Kunstler, was also published in 2005. All these books made bold assertions that we were either at or very near peak-oil production, and massive economic dislocation would soon follow. They have all been soundly proven wrong by subsequent events that followed the publication of their work.

To consider just how embellished the whole notion of peak oil would become, consider the commentary below by Mr. Kunstler, and consider the degree to which these

---

19 Paul Roberts, *The End of Oil: On the Edge of a Perilous New World* (New York, NY: Houghton Mifflin Company, 2004); Jeremy Leggett, *The Empty Tank: Oil, Gas, Hot Air, and the Coming Global Financial Catastrophe* (Random House Publishing Group, 2005.)

comments constitute hyperbole. In a speech he made at the meeting of the Second Vermont Republic in the fall of 2005, he offered the following memorable lines:

> We are at or near the all-time maximum global oil-production peak. We do not have to run out of oil to find ourselves in trouble. When world demand for oil exceeds the world's ability to produce oil, the complex systems we depend on will destabilize…
>
> At the same time, we will be tempted to join a worldwide scramble for the world's remaining oil— most of which belongs to countries whose people don't like us—and the nature of this contest may be very violent. *Our suburbs will prove to be a huge liability. They represent the greatest misallocation of resources in the history of the world. The project of suburbia represents a set of tragic choices because it is a living arrangement with no future. And that future is now here in the form of the peak oil predicament.* (emphasis added).[20]

For a short time in the 2005–2008 period, it seemed like Mr. Kunstler and other similarly minded writers might have indeed turned out to be economic prophets. It was not to be. The price of a barrel of crude oil breached one hundred dollars in the open world market by January 2008. By that

---

20 Remarks by James Howard Kunstler at the meeting of the Second Vermont Republic on October 28, 2005.

summer, the price of oil would surge past $145 per barrel, but it would not last. While it seemed for months that each new trading day brought new record highs for crude oil on the New York and London exchanges, the price per barrel of oil would plunge after the bankruptcy of Lehman Brothers, Inc., and the subsequent financial crisis induced a deepening of the ongoing recession. While prices would soon recover, they would not reach the zenith of 2008 and have not to this day. Even though it seemed that one-hundred-dollars-per-barrel oil would become a fixture of economic life, as Brent Crude, which is usually deferred to as the international benchmark for the price of crude in the global market, remained over one hundred dollars per barrel from 2009 through mid-2014, this elevated price did not preclude an uptick in economic activity starting in January 2011.[21] The seemingly endless persistence of crude in excess of one hundred dollars begged the question as to whether we were actually nearing the point in time where we would max out on the daily production of oil in the international markets. Are we at the peak, where production will decline from here on out, or at best flat line for a decade or two, then enter a fatal decline?

---

21 While the economy is indeed growing, notwithstanding historically elevated crude-oil prices, the author does not believe that high oil prices are the cause of the lackluster US economic performance. The mediocre US economic growth record since June 2009 is more likely due to a convergence of factors such as the retiring of the baby boomer generation, slow recovery from the 2008 financial crisis (which had absolutely nothing to do with elevated oil prices), and poor economic policies of the current presidential administration and a complicit US Congress.

The short answer is no. The events of the past seven years have proven that we are not at peak crude-oil production, and frankly I'm not sure we are even near it. A funny thing happened along the way to peak oil. As the price of a barrel of oil rose, it became commercially viable to extract oil and gas found in shale-rock formation—commonly referred to as "tight oil" in energy circles. What a shock to find that increased production would actually follow a sustained rise in prices that, in turn, led to a sustained rise in profitability. We usually refer to enhanced profit incentive driving more production for what is in high demand as Economics 101. Drilling techniques and technologies that were too expensive at sixty, seventy, or eighty dollars per barrel became very viable at ninety and one hundred dollars. Even as prices have collapsed to the mid-twenty-dollars-per-barrel range in the last eighteen months, drillers managing hydraulic fracture wells have become immensely more efficient, so production increases have held the lower topline revenue fetched by a barrel of crude oil. For now, peak oil remains but a theory, with only minimal empirical support.

The aim of this chapter will be to explore the particulars of the peak-oil theory in detail and then do a quick survey of the adherents to this near-religion, starting with the books already previously noted, as they represent the classic exaggeration that surrounds the entire peak-oil train of thought. In the latter-mentioned work, *The Empty Tank*, the author even went so far as to predict outright economic calamity as a result of hitting peak oil sometime in 2010, with a depression to follow; one the author even asserts would be worse than the 1930s. As usual, Mr. Kunstler goes even further. He is on record publically predicting widespread economic and political unrest, the kind of which would call into question whether or not the United States as you know it today would even survive. In public remarks made in 2005, he stated, "I am describing a nation that may not hold together far into the [twenty-first] century. I would like to be wrong about this, but it [is] hard to look at the big picture and come up with a different set of conclusions."[22] He went on to quote his own book when he said:

> But in the Long Emergency all bets are off for politics, economics, and social cohesion. Turbulence with be the rule *and we will have to do our best to make sure that the just prevail over the wicked, and that the weak are not trampled, and that the best that was in us as a people can somehow be rescued from the dumpster of memory* (emphasis added).[23]

Was there something in the drinking water in the early and mid-2000s? At the time, it seemed like an avalanche of emboldened left-of-center writers were all thinking the same apocalyptic thoughts about the coming energy crisis and the end of civilization that was to follow. If the underpinnings of the oil-scarcity intellectual movement were present since the

---

22 Remarks by James Howard Kunstler at the meeting of the Second Vermont Republic on October 28, 2005.
23 Ibid.

early 1970s, the mid-2000s had the feeling of a "big bang" for the resurgence of this theory. As the notion of limits to growth underpins the idea of peak-oil production, discussion of the intellectual notions of finite resources is warranted. This book will demonstrate that the notion of permanent shortage, as advocated by the peak-oil intellectual contingent, has not come to pass and is not likely to do so anytime soon.

Once we've gone through a synopsis of the peak-oil theory, the mission of this work will be to aggressively confront it. This book is most certainly not intended to merely survey various schools of thought on the matter of energy and raw-material resource abundance. As I stated earlier in the introduction, this book is an uncompromising assault on the whole notion resource scarcity insofar as it is often asserted to mean permanent shortage. The recent events of the past decade should disabuse these notions once and for all. Human ingenuity is proving to be a mighty and powerful force for procuring the materials we need for our modern life.

At this juncture, a discerning reader may ask, "Why take on only three writers on the subject, as there are certainly many others on the peak-oil bandwagon?" The answer is that I am, in fact, attempting to confront all those who pedal peak oil's wears. But since these particular writers made predictions of doom a decade ago that have turned out to be utterly false and have proven to be anything but prescient, it is worth calling them out specifically. Each book by these authors has scores of like-minded writers cited in their bibliographies. By challenging these books, the themes they espouse, and all the sources they cite to make their case, I am, in fact, challenging the whole lot of them. The time for courteous discourse on the matter of energy abundance and the correct policy to exploit that abundance has come and gone. We now live in an era where we cannot even get a pipeline finalized between two sovereign nations to bring crude from the Canadian oil sands to the vast US market where it is needed because the Obama administration is so beholden to thinking along the lines of Kunstler, Leggett, and Roberts. We are now at a point where the progrowth lobby (of which I consider myself a member) must increase the volume regarding the facts of what is occurring regarding energy abundance. The facts have been and are likely to continue to favor our arguments. Blindly following the peak-oil religion will most certainly result in uninformed public policy.

What Is Peak Oil Theory Anyway, and Why Should I Care?

As already alluded to earlier in this book, the theory "peak oil" was originally espoused in the mid-1950s by Shell Oil geologist Marion King Hubbert to reflect the point in time when aggregate, worldwide oil production would reach its maximum level, to be followed by an inexorable and continuous decline in production.[24] Publication No. 95 is the technical paper written by Hubbert in 1956 that depicts what

---

24 M. King Hubbert, *Nuclear Energy and the Fossil Fuels*, Publication No. 95 (Houston, TX: Shell Development Company, Exploration, and Production Research Division, June 1956), 22–23.

would become known in the next fifty years as "Hubbert's Peak" or "peak oil."[25]

The essential prediction of this theory is that based on estimated known global oil reserves in 1956 (1.25 *trillion* barrels) and assuming the 1956 global production rate increases by 2.5 times, the maximum rate of production would be achieved in approximately the year 2000. In this paper, Hubbert fully expected that the maximum rate of production would fluctuate and have the potential to make the anticipated peak year of 2000 subject to change. He wrote:

> In figure 20, the curve has been drawn on the assumption that the maximum rate of production will be about two and one-half times that of the present rate, which places the date of the peak at about the year 2000. *As in the case of coal, variations of this assumed maximum rate will advance or retard the date of the culmination* (emphasis added).[26]

Hence it is clear Mr. Hubbert did not intend for the year 2000 to be some hard-and-fast occurrence to be predicted with the same precision as an astrophysicist can predict the next solar eclipse. Rather he understood the nature of his mathematical calculations was inherently based upon assumptions about information he would not have at the time he made the initial predictions. The best he could do was make educated

---

25 Ibid.

26 Ibid., 22.

projections based on trends that had preceded 1956, and he acknowledged as much.

Indeed nearly a decade and a half after the year 2000, global production has still not peaked,[27] and it is not expected to peak anytime soon. While crude-oil production may fall as a share of all fossil-fuel consumption, this will have more to do with the stunning rise in the worldwide production of natural gas, including massive increases in US natural-gas production in the coming years. The current estimates are that crude-oil production will continue to increase globally through the year 2035.[28]

However, this dynamic alone does not mean his predictions were ultimately without merit. In fact, he made similar predictions about the potential peak of US oil production with uncanny precision. The same technical paper asserting that a year 2000 peak for oil production worldwide made a similar prediction that US domestic oil production would peak in 1970.

This is precisely what happened. Between 1970 and 2008, annual US domestic oil production would indeed fall

---

27 As of Q3 and Q4 2015, global oil production had reached a record 96 million barrels per day. See International Energy Agency (IEA), *Oil Market Report*, Highlights (January 19, 2016).

28 IEA, *World Energy Outlook 2013 Fact Sheets*. Specifically the IEA notes that the source of the increase in production is coming from unconventional sources, such as shale-rock formations known as "tight oil," which were deemed uneconomical only a few short years ago. Conventional wells have indeed reached their peak as they continue to decline in terms of share of total oil output. Ibid.

by nearly 50 percent.[29] In 1970, US crude-oil production reached a heady pace of nearly ten million barrels per day.[30] That number would fall to a bit over five million barrels of crude per day by the summer of 2008.[31] While the downward slope of the curve between 1970 and 2008 was not as steep as Hubbert's curve would have suggested, it was nevertheless a sharp drop in production over a sustained period of almost forty years. Indeed by the mid-2000s, Mr. Hubbert's predictions of 1956 were beginning to look increasingly ominous where crude-oil production was concerned. If he was so spot on with his predictions of the state of US oil production post-1970, it seemed only a matter of time before his production-peak theory would be validated on a global basis.

What would it mean for Western civilization if we had truly reached the peak? The first manifestation that we have reached, or are about to reach, the top crude-oil production on a global basis will be a massive spike in the price of a barrel of crude. The summer of 2008 is a perfect illustration. We had heard for years from many analysts that there had not been a significant new discovery since Prudhoe Bay, Alaska, and without a major new discovery, we were looking at a fixed and known quantity of technically recoverable oil and could

---

29 US Energy Information Administration, *Annual Energy Review 2011* Figure 5.1b, 119. In reviewing this figure, it is easily discernable that, according to the EIA, US production of crude oil peaked nearly exactly in the years 1970–1971, just as Hubbert predicted. The 1970 peak is only now being seriously challenged—forty-six years later.

30 Ibid.

31 Ibid.

extrapolate when existing fields would be exhausted, given current and likely future extraction rates. One will recall that the price of a barrel of crude first hit $100 in March of 2008 and would go on to rise to $147 per barrel by midsummer of that year.[32]

While the price spike of 2008 was certainly one of the sharpest in history—very disruptive and economically pain-ful—it would only be a mild foreshadowing of what would come in the event we actually reach the maximum level of crude-oil production worldwide. Extrapolating the potential price spike that would accompany peak oil is almost so easy a third grader could do it. Think back to the oil embargo of 1972–1974. During that period, the price of a barrel of oil *quadrupled*! Certainly, if we truly reach the peak crude-oil production rate, such that there is simply no more additional oil to be extracted in a manner that would be higher than the extraction rate of the preceding day, then prices would very likely see *at least* a fourfold increase in the price per bar-rel. If we take 2014's price of Brent Crude, which had been averaging about $110 per barrel until the price collapsed, and multiply it by 4, we get a $440 per barrel—very, very quickly. Who's to say how high the price would actually rise?

The point is that there is a relatively recent historical precedent for the quadrupling of petrol prices based on short-ages (albeit man-made ones), so this outcome in the event of peak oil is a virtual sure bet for the period immediately

---

32 US Energy Information Administration (EIA) website tracking daily spot prices for West Texas Intermediate (WTI) Crude from 1986 to 2014.

following the production peak. We can only speculate on how high the price per barrel would ultimately go from then on. If you want to get an idea of the economic impact of such price increases, then imagine what would happen to your household budget in the event you started paying ten to twelve dollars per gallon for gasoline. Multiply that by one hundred million households in the United States and another one hundred million in Europe, and you see that things get ugly very fast.

Were we to actually arrive at peak-oil production today, this outcome is nearly assured because there is no ready alternative to gasoline and diesel fuel for powering a motor vehicle. Switching from gasoline or diesel to natural gas or electricity will take a very long time to ramp up. How many liquefied natural gas and electric stations have you stopped by lately on a recent road trip? Stepping away from gasoline will take time, perhaps even a generation. So is this eventual peak-oil scenario what we are stuck with? What follows is a chronicling of the reasons that this outcome is not likely in the near term (pre-2050).

WHAT ULTIMATELY HAPPENED AND WHAT TO MAKE OF THE PEAK-OIL ALARMISTS

Just when it seemed like the doomsayers were about to have their moment, hydraulic fracture came. Suddenly this curve is becoming more outdated as increasingly sharp increases in US crude-oil production since 2009 has US daily oil production on a path to become the world's largest crude-oil producer by 2017.[33] The United States has not led the world in crude-oil production for a half a century, and the prospect of having that crown returned, even if only for a decade or so, is something completely unforeseen by virtually every analyst anywhere in the world prior to 2009. For the first time since former president Nixon declared a national objective of energy independence for the nation, the United States is poised to achieve that goal. The International Energy Association (IEA) noted in 2013 as follows:

> *Global energy trade is reoriented from the Atlantic basin to the Asia-Pacific region.* China is becoming the largest oil-importing country; India becomes the largest importer of coal by the early 2020s. *Improved energy efficiency and a boom in unconventional oil and gas production help the United States to move steadily toward meeting almost all of its energy needs (in energy equivalent terms) from domestic resources by 2035* (emphasis added).[34]

The notion of the United States meeting the vast majority of its energy needs through its own domestic resources was simply unthinkable as recently as 2005. In 2006, the United

---

33 International Energy Agency, *World Energy Outlook 2013 Factsheet.* The IEA asserts that the United States will be the world's largest producer of crude oil for much of the time between 2012–2035 through better extraction techniques from existing wells and the recovery of oil through "tight oil" formations through hydraulic-fracture methods.
34 Ibid.

States imported nearly 60 percent of the energy it needed, most of it crude oil. By 2013, that had nearly reversed, and as the IEA notes, the trend is toward much more US energy independence over the next two decades, not less.

Furthermore, in May of 2015, the U.S. Energy Information Administration (EIA) had revised its forecasts for US crude-oil production through the year 2025. The agency predicted production growth through 2016 and notes the forecast is for production growth to continue post 2016 but that it would be uncertain.[35] The update contains three scenarios: one assuming high price, one assuming low price, and one for high oil and gas resource.

In the high-price case, US crude production hits 12 mb/d by 2019 and meets or exceeds that rate through 2025.[36] Under the low oil-price case, production remains at just over 9 mb/d from now through 2025.[37] Clearly the low-price scenario is the more likely, given what has transpired in the global crude-oil markets over the past eighteen months. That said, it is important to remember that even under the current low-price scenario, US crude production is anticipated to remain over 9 mb/d, which is within spitting distance from the 1970 peak. This development is truly astonishing given where production was a decade ago.

---

35 US Energy Information Administration (EIA), *US Crude Production to 2025, Updated Projection of Crude Types* (May 2015), iii.

36 Ibid., 2.

37 Ibid.

Obviously this assumes that there will be additional tight-oil discoveries and that the technology will continue to improve. On that front, the EIA recently put US crude-oil reserves at the highest level since the mid-1970s, with the 2012 estimate being a whopping thirty-three billion barrels—the highest since 1976.[38] The following figure from the EIA is illustrative:

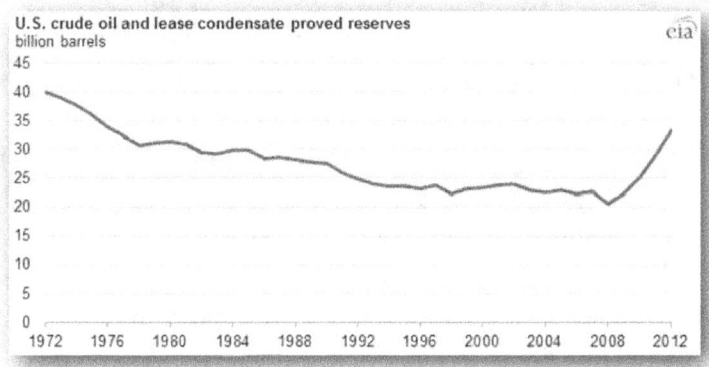

All of this amounts to nothing short of a stunning reversal of a half-century trend that appeared to be irreversible less than a decade ago. The fact that this was completely missed by nearly all analysts anywhere in the world is evidence that, while we know fossil fuels are finite resources, no one knows with absolute certainly when we will exhaust all the coal, oil, and gas within our technological reach and what energy options we will have when that day comes. In addition, no

---

38 EIA, *Crude Oil Reserves at the Start of 2013 Reach Highest Level Since 1976* (April 10, 2014).

one knows for certain what new technological advances will be in place decades from now. The best we have are projections based on available information available at our disposal at the time we make them. What we know will certainly change over time. As our knowledge about oil and natural-gas deposits changes over time, so will the technology available for extracting currently hard-to-reach deposits.

This is precisely where the peak-oil alarmists so completely missed the mark in their analysis. Take *The End of Oil: On the Edge of a Perilous New World*, by Paul Roberts, as an example. He devotes an entire chapter to the notion of depleting oil supplies (chapter 2, "The Last of the Easy Oil"). In that chapter, Roberts surveys all the various major oil fields of the middle of the last decade and proceeds to prognosticate when they are likely to reach peak production. His chapter does not speak in anticipation of any forthcoming new technologies or drilling techniques, but he does make generic references to improved exploration technologies.[39] Roberts did acknowledge the industry's capability to drill horizontally but made no mention of hydraulic fracture when doing so.[40] He goes on to note that even these new exploration technologies have not been sufficient to "halt the long term decline in new discoveries outside of OPEC, where oil producers and international oil companies alike continue to pump out more

---

39 Paul Roberts, *The End of Oil: On the Edge of a Perilous New World* (Houghton Mifflin Company, 2004), 57.
40 Ibid., 55.

oil than they can replace through exploration."[41] The chapter then proceeds to opine that "non-OPEC oil production could peak by 2015" and that "OPEC of course, faces a peak of its own—probably sometime in 2025."[42]

Of course events would unfold over the next ten to eleven years that completely upend these assumptions. We are now in a world where US production is increasing year after year (even though it may temporarily decrease in the latter part of the current decade in response to the price collapse), and, as we will see in chapter 6, it nearly matched its 1970 peak of nearly ten million barrels per day, and is likely to average just over 9 mb/d for the next several decades (even if there are some periods where it falls below that level due to low prices driven by over supply). Later chapters will speak to data showing a present-day world where crude oil is produced in such quantities, a major problem of the day is where to store it. Where Roberts bemoans the possibility non-OPEC production would have peaked by now, US production presently over nine million barrels per day, up massively from the 5.5 mb/d rate of a decade ago. Oil traders now lease oil tankers to store excess crude in hopes of being able to sell it later at an acceptable price. This is not an indicator of scarcity. There are EIA scenarios seriously forecasting that US crude production could someday reach over thirteen million barrels

---

41 Ibid. This assertion by Roberts is patently incorrect. As the next chapter will demonstrate, a review of the SEC filings of some of the world's largest oil companies shows many of them, including ExxonMobil, do, in fact, replace reserves at a rate of 100 percent of current production.

42 Ibid., 59.

per day by 2019 if the price of oil were to spike. In the end, Robert's assertions of fear that the depletion picture was getting really ugly turned out to be quite exaggerated.

Tellingly a thorough read of *The End of Oil* reveals a stunning fact about the book. As mentioned earlier, it says little, if anything, about hydraulic fracture and barely touches on horizontal drilling. I have reviewed the index contained in this book multiple times over the course of the decade that I have owned it, and to this day, I have not been able to find the word hydraulic fracture anywhere in the book. As indicated earlier, and as I will remind the reader in chapter 3, hydraulic fracture has been around in its earliest stages since 1947. While it was certainly an unconventional drilling technology at the time Roberts wrote and published his book, not even discussing these technologies is puzzling. Any serious analysis would have at least presented the reader with some background on them, especially given that this book was written more than fifty years after hydraulic fracture was initially developed. As a consequence of underestimating the role of technology, Mr. Roberts is left with being in the dubious position of having made bold predictions a decade ago that turned out to be diametrically opposed to what actually occurred. This egregious miscalculation is due in large part to underestimating the role of technological innovation in drilling techniques that would result in massively increasing US crude-oil and natural-gas production for a generation.

Similarly the prognostications of Jeremy Leggett made in his 2005 book *The Empty Tank: Oil Gas, Hot Air and the Coming Global Financial Catastrophe* are only marginally better than that of Mr. Roberts. At least Leggett has the gumption to formally acknowledge hydraulic fracture and horizontal drilling, as you can find these words in the index to his book. Furthermore Leggett does demonstrate a basic knowledge of the history of the technology by noting that companies such as Halliburton and its contemporaries began using it beginning around 1960.[43] Horizontal, or "directional," drilling is also referenced on the same page.[44] But while Leggett had enough sense to touch on the existence of these technologies, he was dismissive of their eventual impact.

Regarding whether these new recovery techniques would alter the "tipping point"—that is, the point at which peak-oil production has been reached—Leggett cites a former BP executive as asserting that they would be unlikely to do so.[45] In fact, what would happen between 2009 and 2014 is that these newly perfected techniques, which had been around for decades, would lead to a doubling of US oil output in a five-year period—perhaps the most stunning and unanticipated energy development in the history of petroleum as a primary fuel for industrial society. In short, it is clear that Leggett gave much more thought to these unconventional extraction techniques than Roberts did, but he did so through the lens of deep skepticism, so much so that he stuck with his premise that peak oil was at hand and a global economic collapse was

---

43 Jeremy Leggett, *The Empty Tank: Oil, Gas, Hot Air, and the Coming Global Financial Catastrophe* (Random House, 2005), 20.

44 Ibid.

45 Ibid., 40.

sure to follow. While Leggett does not deny the existence of these technologies, he certainly didn't think they altered the peak-oil time frame much.

So just how wrong are Leggett, Kunstler, and Roberts? As noted previously, the International Energy Agency (IEA) is on record asserting in 2013 that the United States of America will be the world's largest crude-oil producer for much of the period to 2035.[46] That means that some sixty to sixty-five years *after* Marion King Hubbert believed the United States would reach peak oil, the United States will be leading the world in the production of crude oil. Leggett's and Roberts's predictions were, in 2005, that the US production peak was long past, and the global peak just around the corner. Fast-forward ten years, and you find international markets awash in crude-oil supplies, with US production surging beyond an oilman's wildest dreams. Roberts, Leggett, and Kunstler, it appears, had it exactly backward. Conventional oil production had peaked, and the cost of getting the unconventional shale oil was prohibitive at years 1980, 1990, or 2000 prices. Then comes a major price spike of the mid- and late 2000s, and suddenly these technologies become cost effective, and extracting shale oil becomes economical. The initial adjustment in the summer of 2008 was very painful, as we hit four dollars per gallon gas for the first time. But from that point, the price for a gallon of gas stabilized until late 2014, when the price per barrel began to plummet. Now we stand at the beginning of 2016, with gas-price averages less than half what they were in 2008. Incomes have crept

---

46 International Energy Agency, *World Energy Outlook 2013 Factsheet.*

up (much too slowly, one might argue), making the inflation-adjusted price of a gallon of gas more affordable in 2015 than at any time in the past ten years. Even as prices collapse in 2014–2016, shale drillers are getting ever more efficient, and the cost of producing a barrel of oil is declining, along with the global prices. To be sure, there will come a point when the price per barrel gets low enough for long enough that shale drillers can't operate profitably. Over time, however, as prices creep upward again, the drillers will return—the oil is there to be extracted at the right price. For now, the shale drillers continue to weather the price storm, and production remains elevated, with most of the gains coming from the tight formations

One can only wonder aloud at what the peak-oil advocates must have been thinking on January 19, 2016, when the International Energy Agency (IEA) issued its monthly oil market report for that month. The second paragraph of the report reads, "Persistent oversupply, bloated inventories and a slew of negative economic news pressured prices so that by mid-January crude oil touched 12 year lows."[47] This turn of events is the precise opposite of what was predicted by peak-oil authors a decade ago. There is so much supply on the market today that the price of a barrel of crude even touched the mid-twenty-dollar range in January when it was over one hundred dollars per barrel eighteen months ago. We are not running out; we are awash in crude.

---

47 International Energy Agency (IEA) Summary of its Oil Market Report for January 2016 found at: http://www.iea.org/newsroomandevents/news/2016/january/iea-releases-oil-market-report-for-january.html. Issued January 19, 2016.

Perhaps the most damning fact debunking Leggett and Roberts is what happened to crude-oil prices in the spring of 2014. Six years after crude lurched to its highest price ever in the summer of 2008, and five years after the commencement of the current economic recovery, crude-oil prices remained soft worldwide. Not even the Russian invasion of the Crimea could ignite a surge in crude prices. Historically a major international incident involving a large oil-producing nation like Russia would result in a large spike in crude prices, but not this time. I'll say it again because it bears repeating— there was a major international incident involving major oil producers in the middle of a worldwide economic expansion six decades after the first warnings of peak oil, and what do we see? We saw crude-oil prices that were roughly 29 percent below their 2008 peak in nominal terms; if you adjust for inflation, the decrease is even bigger. Fast-forward to the end of 2015, and the price had collapsed still further, resting in the high thirty-dollar range for a barrel of crude, a measly 25 percent of the 2008 peak. The resurgence of US crude-oil production to the point where it is seriously challenging Saudi Arabia for the top spot as the largest oil producer on the planet is clearly keeping a lid on prices worldwide. Recall that these two writers, especially Leggett, asserted that by now we would be seeing catastrophic rises in crude-oil prices, lead-ing to a financial collapse.[48] We're still waiting. Leggett then

---

[48] Leggett, chapter 3, 48–49, is where the author concludes that the oil tipping point for peak production will occur around 2005, and the tipping point for both oil and natural gas would be 2015, to be followed by a "steep descent on the other side of the curve." Then in the epilogue, Leggett goes

postulated that after the carnage, the world would embrace "alternative" energy. The day for wind and solar as primary energy sources may indeed be in the offing, but my view is that the day is much further away than conventional wisdom would have you believe.

The fact is that the bet on alternative energy has been a bust in the short run, as the price for these sources is simply not competitive with existing energy sources including fossil fuels. Far from the financial Armageddon that so many like Roberts and Leggett have predicted over the years, we stand on the cusp of a fossil-fuel renaissance that few thought possible only a few short years ago. It is likely to last for decades, and in the case of natural gas and methane hydrates, perhaps even centuries (more on that in chapters 4 and 6).

Certainly this is not to say that crude prices won't rise again in the future—they will. If they rise modestly over time, even with the occasional spike, there will be more and more economic incentives to extract previously difficult to reach "tight oil" or "unconventional oil" from shale-rock formations around the world—and it all started in the United States, the absolute last place anyone would have thought of a decade ago.

At this juncture, it is appropriate to recognize some of the authors who "got it right" at roughly the same point in time that the likes of Roberts and Leggett predicted doom.

---

on to draw the link between declining production and an explosion of prices once investors become aware that the world has reached peak production. See Leggett, 190–191.

In early 2005, I stumbled upon a jewel of a book entitled *The Bottomless Well: The Twilight of Fuel, The Virtue of Waste, and Why We Will Never Run Out of Energy* by Peter W. Huber and Mark P. Mills.[49] It is quite ironic that this book was published in exactly the same time period as the works of Leggett, Roberts, and others, with the irony being that it reached the *exact opposite* conclusion. The book goes into a fair amount of technical engineering detail but spares the reader arcane technocratic analytics. The authors put the hard science in terms easily understandable by the nonengineering layman. A book that would be a "fun read" for a petroleum engineer is also manageable for someone without a geology or engineering background. Because it is likely so few of my fellow Americans are aware of this great book, it is unlikely to become a staple for the must-read summer reading list. I will tell you this: if you care to have at least a basic understanding of the energy science behind fossil fuels and to further understand why the fossil-fuel era is very likely in its infancy rather than its final stages, you need to read this book. If you care about what kind of energy policy your elected officials are embracing with your money, you need to read it. If you're at all concerned with the energy future your children will inherit, you need to read this excellent book by Huber and Mills. As I will demonstrate in the pages that follow, these gentlemen came *far* closer to forecasting what would happen

---

49 Peter W. Huber and Mark P. Mills, *The Bottomless Well: The Twilight of Fuel, The Virtue of Waste and Why We Will Never Run Out of Energy* (Basic Books, 2005).

post 2008 in terms of fossil-fuel production than just about anyone else.

When *The Bottomless Well* first hit the shelves of book stores in 2005, *Business Week* featured it in its weekly book-review column in March of that year. The column by Peter Coy did a nice job of summarizing the main points and even had to acknowledge the plausibility of the main premise of the book—that the world is not running out of raw fuel and that human ingenuity should be at the center of any energy debate.[50] Nevertheless *The Bottomless Well* was very much a contrarian view at the time it was written and published. I've discussed the two books by Roberts and Leggett at length, but there were others of the same intellectual mind-set that the world would soon be running out of oil and other fossil fuels.[51] It seemed, at the time, that many authors were lining up to tell us all the end was nigh.

As you might expect, Huber and Mill's book's overall con-clusion is given away by its title. The authors do not leave you guessing what the book is about. They spend 198 pages mak-ing their case that fossil-fuel energy, including crude oil, will be in abundance for decades to come. They assert that there are "unimaginably large," to use their term, stores of fossil fuels,

---

50 Peter Coy, "Energy Crisis? Phooey," *Business Week*, (March 14, 2005), 23.

51 See David Goodstein, *Out of Gas: The End of the Age of Oil* (W. W. Norton & Co., February 2004). Classic peak-oil thesis asserting that civilization as we know it is destined to end by the close of the twenty-first century unless fossil-fuel dependence is ended; and Kenneth S. Deffeyes, *Beyond Oil: The View from Hubbert's Peak* (Hill and Wang, 2005). This book is a literal recap of the peak-oil theory beginning with Hubbert's analysis, although this work does explicitly acknowledge the prospect of oil shale.

including oil and coal, and they argue the same for uranium, and, most important, they assert that there is virtually no risk of running short. Chapter 11, entitled "Infinite Supply," makes the case that Leggett and Roberts, and others like them, failed to properly grasp, which is that there has been and will continue to be an unrelenting and continuous improvement in the technologies that find and retrieve energy, including oil, resulting in relatively stable energy prices over time.[52]

Interestingly there are several key facts that Huber and Mills cite in the prologue to their book that are worth mentioning. They reference a 1981 *National Geographic* article that predicted $200 per barrel by 2003.[53] The facts would intervene as follows:

> And Americans today are burning more [oil] than ever before.
>
> Most of the new demand for oil was met with imports, but by no means all. US Fields, the oldest in the world with many predating World War I, had been scheduled to run dry by the 1990s—only about 30 billion barrels of "proven reserves" remained

---

52 Huber and Mills, *The Bottomless Well*, 173. On this page, the authors explain how crude is now being extracted in what would have been impossibly difficult locations fifty years ago and expressly note the use of horizontal drilling for retrieval. That Leggett and Roberts either failed to mention such a technique entirely, or downplay its relevance at a time where other authors "got it," tells you everything you need to know about the quality of their analysis.

53 Huber and Mills at p. xvii citing *"Energy: A Special Report in the Public Interest."* National Geographic, February 1981, 2.

in 1979, after a century in which 160 billion barrels (cumulatively) had been pumped out of those same wells. *Nevertheless, in the quarter century since 1979, US wells alone yielded another 67 billion barrels. The big oil fields of Oklahoma had been discovered in 1859; the reserves in those fields were assessed at 12.5 million barrels in 1969. Yet in the next quarter century they yielded 4.5 billion additional barrels"* (emphasis added).[54]

The very powerful point made is that the relentless advancement of extraction technology yielded far more crude-oil production from tired, supposedly soon-to-be exhausted oil wells than many experts predicted. So much for the doomsday predictions from the peak-oil alarmists, who, no doubt, thought their day had come by mid-2008, but technological improvements would stay their day of vindication. They'll have to wait because, as of winter 2015–2016, crude-oil supplies in the United States are at record levels, so much so, there are oil tankers being leased by energy traders to store crude in hopes prices will increase so the oil can be sold later at higher price. The fun of it all is that the Texas Permian basin once again became a top crude-oil producer for the United States by May 2014. Remember that this was the geographical area that was referred to in World War II as the "kettle that kept the Allied military machine moving." This is nearly a decade *after* Huber and Mills published their work! Apparently "the end of oil" will have to wait a few more decades.

---

54 Ibid., xix.

What is instructive about *The Bottomless Well* is that the optimists in the mid-2000s made a much stronger case than the pessimists, and facts have been kind to those who sought to provide a clear-eyed analysis of what our energy prospects were actually going to be. In hindsight, the pessimists look to have been too eager to jump on the cataclysmic bandwagon and peddle doom and gloom. The initiative and ingenuity of the American private industrial sector proved to be a prolific and powerful force. I must admit that in the dark days of 2008, it did indeed look as if the peak-oil canard would rule the day and that our way of life would come under serious stress in very short order.

Those sentiments seem a faded, distant memory now. New predictions, projections, and estimates of renewed American energy dominance are now commonplace. It does appear to me that Huber and Mills were absolutely correct to bet on the stalwart American creativity to bring about and perfect extraction technologies beyond the wildest imagination. Indeed, they were more than right when they argued that the more energy we use, the more we create and that we have a dynamism that will require ever-increasing amounts of energy and the technological prowess to find it—including oil, coal, natural gas, and anything else we need. Perhaps the most telling facet of this new era of oil and gas abundance is the fact that the massive increase in proved reserves and the sharp increase in production has occurred almost exclusively on private lands. The federal government has been a literal bystander to this turn of events and, in some cases, an outright impediment. Federal intransigence will not stop the hydraulic fracture and horizontal drilling freight train, which has left the station and is headed in the direction of abundance for decades to come.

So today we are left on the cusp of a literal energy revolution. For nearly four decades, our proved energy reserves in oil and gas, as well as the production of these fuels, declined steadily, but in the past seven years, we've seen the sharpest reversal in a lifetime.[55] The outlook couldn't be better for the near and intermediate terms, and the longer term gets a little brighter each year as well. Where authors once lined up to tell us we were running out, they have now gone silent or they look for any shred of evidence that gives them the slimmest basis to stay on the peak-oil bandwagon. Old attitudes die hard, and there are those who are not about to let facts get in the way of their ideology. But the facts are getting more and more favorable for those that take the optimistic view that energy abundance is the future and that energy scarcity will have to wait. Huber and Mills represent the views of optimists in the think tanks; then what is the view of the world's most predominant energy companies themselves—those that stand to lose or gain the most from the outcome of the debate? After all, regarding the energy companies, these are the people who "do this for a living"!

---

55 On December 11, 2015, Reuters issued the following press release: *Oil prices slide after IEA warns of further oversupply* (emphasis added). The article went on to note that Brent Crude prices were on track for the lowest weekly close since 2008 (a seven-year low). The point to be made repeatedly is that there is so much oil that crude prices are collapsing as of YE 2015. Prices would continue to collapse to the mid-twenty-dollar-per-barrel range in January 2016 on glut worries.

CHAPTER 2

What Did Major Petroleum Companies Think of Their Long-Term Prospects with the Price Volatility of Recent Years?

———

WHAT BETTER WAY TO ASSESS the outlook of a major, publicly traded energy company than to look at what it is telling its investors in securities and exchange documents? After all, purposefully misleading the investing public in formal SEC disclosures would result in serious legal jeopardy for the company and its senior officers, so they have a good bit of incentive to portray an accurate picture of what the revenue prospects will be in the future—and since they are energy companies, revenue, to a significant extent, will come from the production of oil and gas.

This chapter will survey the SEC filings and other publications issued by the five largest petroleum companies that have publicly traded securities on a major US equities exchange, such as the New York Stock Exchange (NYSE), when crude oil was selling on the world market for one hundred dollars per barrel or more. The discussion will begin with each company's outlook for energy demand in the coming decades and their ability to satisfy that demand with liquid-petroleum-based fuels. The overwhelming theme is that among the major world energy companies, the outlook for energy demand over the next three decades is quite bullish, as is their belief in their own ability to continue increasing petroleum output. From the world's major economic and business entities responsible for supplying the world's energy, you do not hear defeatist peak-oil theory; rather, you hear them tell their shareholders and the public at large that they will be positioned to continue to generate revenue from the production, refinement, and distribution of petroleum products.

Before getting into the detail of the arguments of this chapter, please be advised that in making my arguments, I cover financial data from the SEC filings of the major oil companies. I do this in order to make the point that I do not see any indication from the performance of these companies on which an argument for peak oil can be made. The assertions I make in this chapter are based on my interpretation of what is stated in public filings by these companies. I do not make any representations on whether or not one should purchase shares in any of these companies, and I am not an advocate for any of these organizations in any way. My analysis is purely academic. I do not intend for this chapter to constitute investment advice or market analysis of the likely long-run performance of the shares of any of these companies. With that disclaimer out of the way, let's begin.

ExxonMobil Corporation

ExxonMobil Corporation is a company incorporated under the laws of New Jersey in 1882. Its 2013 Form 10-K contains the following statement in its opening summary:

> Divisions and affiliated companies of ExxonMobil operate or market products in the United States and most other countries of the world. Their principal business is energy, involving exploration for, and production of, crude oil and natural gas, manufacture of petroleum products and transportation and sale of crude oil, natural gas and petroleum products. ExxonMobil is a major manufacturer and marketer of commodity petrochemicals, including olefins, aromatics, polyethylene and polypropylene plastics and a wide variety of specialty products. ExxonMobil also has interests in electric power generation facilities. Affiliates of ExxonMobil conduct extensive research programs in support of these businesses.[56]

From the onset, ExxonMobil's principal business is energy, involving the exploration for fossil fuel, the production of crude oil, and the distribution and sale of finished petroleum products. That, in turn, means a material portion of ExxonMobil's total revenue and net income will be derived

---

56 ExxonMobil Corporation, US Securities and Exchange Commission Form 10-K, 2013, Part I, Item 1. Business.

from the same.[57] Perhaps most important, in the case of ExxonMobil, earnings for the exploration and development are much higher than for the actual refinement and sale of finished products.[58] Therefore, it stands to reason that ExxonMobil has a very high stake in successfully ensuring that it continues to find more and more oil and gas if it wishes to continuing to supply shareholders the earnings to justify a market valuation in the hundreds of billions. In fact, one primary measure of how much ExxonMobil's success in the area of proved reserves is whether or not it is capable of replenishing reserves year in and year out.

Toward this end, ExxonMobil regularly provides shareholders with information on whether or not in the previous reporting year, the company was able to replace reserves

---

57 The 2013 Form 10-K depicts the earnings breakdown for down as follows. Upstream earnings (petroleum and natural-gas exploration and development) were $26,841 million, down $3,054 million from 2012. Higher gas realizations, partially offset by lower liquids realizations, increased earnings by $390 million. Production volume and mix effects decreased earnings by $910 million. All other items, including lower net gains from asset sales, mainly in Angola, and higher expenses reduced earnings by $2.5 billion. On an oil-equivalent basis, production was down 1.5 percent compared to 2012. Ibid., 44. Downstream earnings (the refinement sale of finished Petroleum Products) of $3,449 million decreased $9,741 million from 2012 driven by the absence of the $5.3 billion gain associated with the Japan restructuring. Lower margins, mainly refining, decreased earnings by $2.9 billion. Volume and mix effects decreased earnings by $310 million. All other items, including higher operating expenses, unfavorable foreign exchange impacts, and lower divestments, decreased earnings by $1.2 billion. Petroleum product sales of 5,887 kbd decreased 287 kbd from 2012. US downstream earnings were $2,199 million, down $1,376 million from 2012. Non-US Downstream earnings were $1,250 million, a decrease of $8,365 million from the prior year. Ibid., 46.
58 Ibid.

at a rate that either matched or exceeded production. This is a critical metric in terms of gauging the long-run ability of a petroleum company's ability to generate earnings. In ExxonMobil's case, it has been able to replace proved oil and gas reserves at a rate that exceeded 100 percent of production for twenty-two consecutive years ending in 2014.[59] Clearly, ExxonMobil does not indicate that it lacks the capacity to replace its existing reserves going forward, as it has a multi-decade track record of replenishing reserves at a rate equal to or greater than current production. The notion of peak oil is very much discredited by this ongoing dynamic. According to the alarmists, we were supposed to be at peak-oil production by now, but our largest energy company replaces reserves at a sustainable rate year in and year out.

There are other compelling facts noted in the 2012 annual report worth mentioning, as they offer a basis for refuting the notion that we are running out of oil. The dividend performance of ExxonMobil over time, as well as its share price relative to the market over time, does not suggest a company on the verge of collapse due to oil scarcity.

---

59 Exxon Mobil 2014 Annual Report, Summary and Highlights section. To be fair, ExxonMobile just announced in an SEC filing on Febrtuary 15, 2016, that while it added 1 billion barrels of oil and gas equivalent to its reserves, the reserve replacement ratio for all of 2015 fell to 67 percent of current production, the first time in twenty-two years that the ration was less than 100 percent. As of YE 2015, ExxonMobile had 24.8 billion barrels of oil equivalent in proved reserves, enough to support current production for sixteen years. I believe that this decline in the reserve replacement ratio is driven by the collapse in oil prices making shale gas less economical to extract in the short run. In the same filing, Exxon reported that its ten-year average reserve replacement ration is 115 percent.

Each year, Exxon's financial performance demonstrates its ability to deliver a steadily improving dividend increase to its shareholders, as well as shareholder returns that are better than the overall market for the past two decades. If peak oil were a real threat, does any serious person believe that an oil company would be able to generate steady profits? There are those who say yes because the price spikes that will accompany an increasingly scarce commodity will be so massive that companies such as Exxon will be flooded with cash and profits, so much so that their financial performance will blossom. Without getting into too much detail, let me respectfully disagree. First, if we really are running out, the exploration and development costs for a company like Exxon will skyrocket right along with the price for oil. The company's ability to generate net earnings will be severely impaired by what will become an out-of-control cost structure for their primary "upstream" exploration and recovery businesses. When there is nothing left to discover, there will be only expense and cost, and the business model will collapse. Analysts will see this years before it actually happens. They clearly are not seeing it yet because, as Exxon itself notes, increases and advancements in exploration and recovery technology will put this day long into the future.

In fact, ExxonMobil is so confident that technological improvements will yield increases in production over the next three decades that it forecasts that oil and gas production will continue to grow through 2040 and remain the predominant source of energy worldwide through that time.[60] The annual

---

60 Ibid., "Outlook for Energy."

reports routinely make clear Exxon believes energy demand will steadily increase, and oil and gas will be the largest contributors to the energy mix, with natural gas replacing coal as the second-largest component and renewables still less than 20 percent of the overall mix. The unmistakable conclusion is that Exxon, as stated in its annual SEC filings, sees oil and gas as the predominant energy sources for the next thirty-plus years, very much in line with the EIA and IEA projections. The company makes repeated assertions that technology will be determinative in unlocking unconventional sources of oil and gas, which will play an ever-increasing role in their production. Peak oil will simply have to wait.

Clearly Exxon Mobil is maintaining that there is good reason to assume that there will be sustainable earnings in the long run from existing Exxon businesses, albeit with periodic volatility. Exxon president and CEO Rex Tillerson concluded the 2012 letter to shareholders by asserting the company is committed to creating long-term value. The letter starts by noting all the competitive advantages the company has regarding oil exploration, refinement, and distribution. It is obvious to the reader that Mr. Tillerson believes oil and gas will be a revenue and profit driver for the company for a long time to come.

Chevron Corporation

The San Francisco–based Chevron Corporation is the nation's second-largest petroleum company. Though it is not as large as ExxonMobil, it is still one of the world's largest global petroleum-exploration and refining companies. Like

ExxonMobil, Chevron derives a massive revenue and net-income base from the exploration and development of crude oil and natural gas—or the "upstream" revenue activity, as it is commonly referred to in industry lexicon. Additionally, as with other major oil companies, Chevron believes it will be able to deliver additional shareholder revenue well into the future with increases in the production and extraction of crude oil and natural gas, and the company has invested billions in some of the world's most complex fossil-fuel energy projects. Let's examine the facts.

In the 2013 letter to shareholders, chairman and CEO John S. Watson chronicles the company's position as one of the most efficient upstream players and then outlines the massive investments being made for the exploration, development, and extraction of crude oil and natural gas. He writes:

Throughout 2013 our major businesses generated strong operating results. In the upstream, we ranked No. 1 in earnings per barrel relative to our peers for the fourth continuous year. We began production of the Angola liquefied natural gas (LNG) plant and achieved first oil from the Papa-Terra project offshore Brazil. In 2013 we also advanced our two world-class LNG projects in Western Australia. Construction at Gorgon is approximately 75 percent complete, and construction at Wheatstone is approximately 25 percent complete. Over the next four years we anticipate 15 project startups with a Chevron investment of more than $1 billion each, including two key deepwater projects in the US Gulf of Mexico—Jack/ St. Malo and Big Foot, which are expected to come online in 2014 and 2015 respectively.

We continued to add resources to our portfolio through both exploration and target acquisitions in 2013. The success rate of our exploration wells was nearly 59 percent, and we added crude oil and natural gas resources through discoveries in 10 countries. We grew our portfolio of opportunities with a new operating interest in the Kurdistan region of Iraq, new acreage in the Bight Basin offshore of South Australia, and finalized agreements to pursue unconventional resources in Argentina as well as assume full partnership of the Kitmat LNG plant and Pacific Trail Pipeline in Canada. We also successfully completed the first phase of our Duvernay Shale program in Canada. *We added approximately 800 million barrels of net oil-equivalent proved reserves, replacing almost 85 percent of production in 2013. The company's three-year average reserve replacement ration is 123 percent of net oil equivalent production.* (emphasis added).[61]

Does this sound like a company in retreat? Does this sound like a company telling its owners that it will have difficulty meeting energy demand with the production of crude oil and natural gas? Did you catch the highlighted section, where

---

61 2013 Letter to Stockholders, President and CEO John S. Watson, 2013 Chevron Corporation Annual Report to Stockholders.

over the past three years, the company has replaced 123 percent of net oil equivalent production? Does that sound like a peak-oil problem? Remember from chapter 1, according to Hubbert's initial projections back in the 1950s, we were supposed to have reached peak oil around the year 2000. Fourteen years later, major oil companies are having no difficulty replacing reserves with amounts either equal to or greater than the previous year's production—on average. In fact, Chevron is so sure of its capabilities in developing oil and gas resources that it has allocated a $39.8 billion capital and exploratory budget.[62] As with ExxonMobil, Chevron has experienced strong financial results over the past few years, with dividends offered to shareholders and the stock pricing rising smartly over time.

These financial results are an unmistakable indicator that for Chevron, all the fundamentals, including the needed reserves for the future, are lined up nicely and properly reflected in its share price. The basic premise of this chapter is that if peak oil were truly an imminent threat, you would see it reflected in the share price, since the upstream expenses would be exploding as the company desperately searched for resources that are no longer there or can be found only in ever fewer quantities. Since Chevron is able to replace reserves at a rate higher than existing production, scarcity is clearly not the case. What exactly is Chevron's view of future energy demand and the portion of oil and gas that will meet that demand into the future? As with other major players,

---

62 Ibid.

Chevron's proved reserves have been increasing at a rate that, over time, is replacing more than 100 percent of current production.[63] Again, it is worth reiterating that over the past five years, the reserve replacement rate has been 100 percent—not exactly a harbinger of the "end is nigh" peak-oil hysteria.

All of this culminates in a company earnings capacity that is one of the largest capital-generating machines in the world. Earnings for the company have risen steadily over the past several years, and as was the case with Exxon, the upstream activities (oil and gas exploration and development) have been by far the biggest revenue and profit generators for Chevron.[64] The final nail in the coffin for the peak oilers is the amount of money that Chevron has budgeted for the exploration and development of crude oil and natural gas.[65]

Of the $41.9 billion in total expenditures for 2013, charts in the 2013 annual report show that $37.9 billion (90 percent) of that total was allocated toward activities that are for the purpose of exploring and developing crude oil and natural gas (the upstream activities).[66] So let's ask an obvious question: If peak oil is a real threat, why is Chevron spending 90 percent of its capital and exploratory expenditures looking for something

---

63 Ibid.,13. The annual report predictably then goes on to hedge and explain all the risk factors that might render the projection inaccurate. But the historical track record is that absent major unforeseen contingencies, this company produces a steady but massive level of oil equivalent year in and year out.

64 As the financial summary states, the income from exploration and development of oil and gas is usually many times higher than the net income from the downstream sale of petroleum products.

65 Ibid., 20.

66 Ibid., 20.

we are supposed to be running out of? Any word from Leggett, and Roberts? Chevron has a fiduciary duty to its stockholders to generate revenue and net income that can be returned to them in dividends or be held as retained earnings for further investment in the business. Would a company with global operations for the exploration and development of crude oil and natural gas be investing tens of billions in that endeavor if it had the hard information that we are about to run out of oil—that there is no more additional oil to be found? To be sure, all major oil companies are in the process (as of late 2015 and early 2016) of cutting back significantly on big capital expenditures related to exploration and development. But that is because the price collapse of crude in the international markets has made them temporarily infeasible financially. First, this will change as soon as prices rebound, and second, this has nothing to do with peak-oil driven scarcity. To the contrary, the current cutback on exploration and development is driven solely by the global crude oil glut—period.

I don't know about you, but I'm going to remain skeptical on the peak-oil theories and divert to a point I've made repeatedly and will continue to make. And that is that were we to be truly at peak production, major oil companies would see their capital and exploratory budgets explode in a desperate attempt to find oil and gas that is no longer there, or else these budgets would shrivel to near nothing if the companies like Chevron come into hard information that there is no more crude oil to be found. Then and only then do you have a clear private-sector indicator of when the end is near for the petroleum age. At this point, there is no such indication.

ConocoPhillips

While ConocoPhillips is certainly not of the size and magnitude of either ExxonMobil or Chevron in terms of revenue or net income, it is still one of the world's largest publically traded companies and a major player in the petroleum industry. Like the others, ConocoPhillips is very dependent on successfully finding, extracting, and transporting crude oil and natural gas to buyers around the globe. Like the others, ConocoPhillips has a worldwide operation in a multiplicity of countries. When the day comes that we truly reach peak-oil production, the business model for ConocoPhillips will either have changed to meet the new world order, or the company will be defunct. What follows is a brief discussion on the business outlook of ConocoPhilips as told by the company to its stockholders via its most recent annual report and 10-K filing.

On one salient point, ConocoPhillips differs from the other large petroleum companies in that it derives its revenue nearly exclusively from upstream exploration and development activities and completely divested its downstream businesses in 2012.[67] Think about that for a moment. If peak oil is truly upon us as the doomsayers contend, then Conoco Philips just made the biggest business and investment blunder in history by getting out of every other business *but* the exploration and extraction of crude oil and natural gas. Wouldn't this bet have

---

67 2013 Letter to Shareholders from President and CEO Ryan M. Lance, pegging the divestiture of downstream businesses and assets beginning in April 2012 with the sale of noncore assets into 2013. The letter asserts that ConocoPhillips is now the world's largest independent E&P Company.

resulted in a calamity in the share price for ConocoPhillips? While the share price of ConocoPhillips did indeed fall from a peak of $85.73 in May of 2014 to just under $35 by late January of 2016, the reason cannot be attributed to the lack of oil because it is widely known the world is flooded with too much of the resource. It stands to reason that when the retail price of crude collapses by two-thirds, an oil company's share price may well do the same. In my view, the behavior of this company's share price is consistent with the current glut and the impact it has on the company's revenue stream.

a) PRODUCTION AND RESERVES

A review of ConocoPhillips's 2014 Annual Report and 10-K suggests that even as the price of crude started to plummet in 2014, the company was able to keep production and reserve replacement on track. In my view, if the aim is to examine an oil company's performance to discern whether there are indicators of peak oil, then these are two primary metrics to focus on.

b) RESERVE REPLACEMENT

As of YE 2014, the reserve replacement ratio for ConocoPhillips was 124 percent.[68] It was 179 percent for 2013 and 156 percent for 2012.[69] This outstanding performance is perhaps

---

68 ConocoPhillips 2014 Annual Report, 9.
69 Ibid.

the strongest indicator of all that ConocoPhillips will be positioned to keep production at desired levels and will be a significant revenue generator for years and years to come. Certainly managing through the price volatility and the current glut will pose significant challenges; nevertheless, the ability to replace reserves at a pace that exceeds the rate of current production ensures many years of steady output, revenue, and profits. I see no sign of peak oil here.

c) Financial Performance through 2015

For 2014, ConocoPhillips reported $6.9 billion in annual earnings, with $5.1 billion in cash or cash equivalents.[70] This performance, along with the continuation of paying out dividends to shareholders, does not portend an end-of-oil scenario for this company. As asserted many times before, one surefire indicator of when we really do reach the end of oil is that capital budgets for these companies will explode in frenzied last-ditch efforts to get at what little there is left, or they will recognize the futility of it all and fold the shop. Neither is present with ConocoPhillips. We have a steady, well-run business managing through some tough market conditions by making sound and robust investments in the future of oil and natural gas. It is also worth mentioning at this point that unlike many of the other major oil companies, ConocoPhillips has done well to capitalize on the unconventional shale oil and gas production. Finally, while

---

70 Ibid., 2.

ConocoPhillips did have to significantly cut its dividend in late 2015 (and others will likely have to follow suit), this is a result of the financial pressure put on by the price collapse, which is a direct and proximate result of the global oil supply glut—not peak-oil-related scarcity.

British Petroleum (BP)

And now we get to the one company least positioned to support my argument, but due to its market presence, it bears analysis nonetheless. Here we have a very old petroleum company that over the past twenty years has sent mixed marketing signals as to its commitment to the petroleum business. I remember vividly the advertising campaign a decade and a half ago run by BP in an attempt to rebrand their initials BP from British Petroleum to a more eco-friendly "Beyond Petroleum." It is understandable that any major corporation of any kind will periodically want to freshen up its brand image and change its name, logo, or other trademark intellectual materials in order to remain relevant in the marketplace. However, to toy with the idea that a petroleum company wants to get "beyond petroleum" raises the prospect that it struggles to figure out what it is trying to do when it gets up in the morning. Its operating results reflect as much.

We could go on ad infinitum about the atrocious business decisions that led to the Deep Water Horizon explosion, which killed everyone on the platform and led to one of the worst Gulf of Mexico petroleum spills in history of deepwater oil exploration. We won't because it is not necessary. I merely bring it up because I want the reader to understand that I view BP as an outlier whose financial and operating results do not necessarily reflect the future of the petroleum industry but rather depict the travails of a specific company's struggle to find its place in a very competitive industry in an ever-changing world. With that said, on with the survey of BP results.

As with the others, we analyze performance based on what is being presented to shareholders in materials accompanying legal flings with the SEC, so we start by looking at the most recent full year reporting as noted in the 2014 Annual Report.

a) PRODUCTION

BP's production of crude oil, condensate, natural-gas liquids (NGLs), and natural gas (collectively converted into "barrels of oil equivalent") has fallen each and every year from 2010 through 2014.[71] In 2010, BP production was a bit over 3.8 million barrels of oil equivalent per day, which dropped each and every year through 2014, where it landed at 3.151 million barrels of oil equivalent per day.[72]

b) RESERVE REPLACEMENT

For 2014, the reserve replacement ratio for BP was 63 percent, down from 129 percent for 2013 and 77 percent for 2012.[73]

---

71 BP Annual Report and Form 20-F, 2014, 19
72 Ibid.
73 Ibid.

This is a metric where BP has underperformed when compared to its peers, averaging roughly 95 percent of current production since 2010.[74] Since this is the only major play to trend below the 100 percent mark, it should be viewed as an outlier and not the harbinger of a trend.

c) FINANCIAL PERFORMANCE, 2010–2015

While profits were down materially in 2014 for BP due to adjustments related to impairments relating to the Gulf of Mexico spill, over the past three years (2012–2014) BP has netted over $38.2 billion attributable to shareholders.[75] That is an average of over $12.7 billion per year. While the next couple of years will not likely match that performance due to the collapse in crude prices worldwide, the fact is that the financial performance of the company is quite viable, notwithstanding the ball and chain for impairments related to past debacle at the Gulf of Mexico. For 2015, BP reported its largest ever annual loss, but again, that was driven by the collapse in the price of crude on world markets, which itself is driven by too much supply. Peak-oil scarcity is not a factor in BPs financial results.

Perhaps the best indicator of long-run viability for the oil and gas industry in the eyes of BP senior executives is illustrated by what is said in the "Market Outlook" portion of the annual report. In the section on oil and natural gas, the

---

74 Ibid.
75 Ibid., 22.

assertion is made that oil and gas are likely to comprise the majority of energy consumption through 2035 and that these two fuels will "play a significant part" in meeting energy demand for several decades.[76] They write:

> Oil and natural gas are likely to play a significant part in meeting demand for several decades. We believe these energy sources will represent about 54 percent of total energy consumption in 2035. Even under the International Energy Agency's most ambitious climate policy scenario (the 450 scenario), oil and gas would still make up 49 percent of the energy mix in 2030 and 43 percent in 2040.
>
> We expect oil to remain the dominant source for transport fuels, accounting for almost 90 percent of demand in 2035.[77]

In short, if the executives at BP and the analysts at the IEA are correct in their forecasts, twenty years from now, you will very likely still be gassing up your car or pickup on the way to work and on your road trips. This is not a peak-oil scenario and to cloud the policy debate with the kinds of doomsday assertions that we've seen regularly over the past forty years does no one any favors.

---

76 Ibid., 11
77 Ibid.

ROYAL DUTCH SHELL

Shell Oil is one of the most profitable business ventures on the planet, a primary competitor with ExxonMobil. Its 2014 results were robust across a wide variety of metrics. Oil and gas expiration are front-and-center sources of energy for this century-old company and will be for decades to come. Below is a snapshot of key metrics for the company.

a) PRODUCTION

Daily production volumes for Shell were down slightly in 2014 versus 2013 but still over three million barrels of oil equivalent per day (including crude oil, natural-gas liquids, synthetic crude oil, and bitumen) or 1.124 billion for the entire year.[78] The 2014 figure was very close to the 1.168 figure for 2013 and the 1.194 billion BOE for 2012.[79] The trend is steady production, and the outlook is the same for the long term.

b) PROVED RESERVES

The level of proved reserves for 2014 was just under 13.1 billion barrels of oil equivalent, down slightly from 13.9 BOE for 2013 and 13.5 for 2012.[80] Shell has demonstrated continued acumen in keeping proved reserves at a constant level,

---

78 Shell Annual Report and Form 20-F 2014, 11, 20.

79 Ibid., 11.

80 Ibid.

ensuring steady production for years to come. For example, the exploration drive for 2014 yielded ten notable discoveries around the world, which may well act as an important source of oil and gas for decades to come.[81] It is worth remembering that this statement is being made in connection with legal filings required of public companies. Misstating or misrepresenting reserve projections without justification can yield significant liability for any energy company. Shell has run into trouble with reserve statements in 2004, where reserves were overstated, and the company was fined by the British Financial Services Authority (FSA) and had to contend with multiple civil lawsuits on the matter. Therefore I assume the company is exercising higher-than-average care and diligence in making statements in connection with reserves and discoveries. If significant problems were foreseen regarding reserve replenishment that may have a bearing on the company's stock price, your author is quite certain that would be carefully vetted in these filings. With this said, I believe Shell's outlook is another indicator that the peak-oil theory is baseless at the present time.

c) FINANCIAL PERFORMANCE, 2012–2014

Shell's financial performance over recent years has been very solid. For 2014, Shell earned $19 billion versus $17 billion in 2013.[82] The company is paying a robust level of dividends

---

81 Ibid., 9.

82 Ibid., 7

to shareholders. For 2014, the company paid $12 billion in dividends, and for 2013, it paid $11 billion.[83] These are not indicators of a company in steep decline due to the fact that we are running out of oil. In fact, the primary risk factor for this company, as with all energy companies at the end of 2015, is, as I've noted previously, the collapsing prices that are a result of the massive oil glut that is the direct and proximate result of huge successes in discovering large "tight oil" or nontraditional oil supplies and getting them to market in huge quantities. The much lower prices for a barrel of oil will, no doubt, place stress on even a stalwart company like Shell, but over the long run, supply and demand equalize, and the price will stabilize. When the prices ultimately do rise again, production advances will resume for reasons I have already discussed.

To summarize this chapter, we see that large energy companies still have oil and gas as key components for their revenue-generating portfolios and are indicating they will do so for at least the next two decades. Energy demand and consumption are expected to rise modestly along with economic growth, and oil and gas will fuel that growth as a large source of energy through 2040. Oil-based liquids will be the predominant transportation fuel for at least the next twenty years. Remember that a decade ago, we were told by the doomsayers that we would be running out of oil by now and facing economic calamity. They have been proven plain wrong, as the facts have landed diametrically opposite of what

---

83 Ibid.

was predicted by the alarmists. The facts, as summarized by the IEA, major oil producing companies, and the US Energy Administration Association, all point in the direction of oil abundance for the next several decades versus the chronic, debilitating shortages that were predicted ten years ago.

Will "Fracking" (Hydraulic Fracture) and Horizontal Drilling Live Up to Their Long-Term Promise over the Long Run?

————

As the manuscript for this book was being finalized in early 2016, the price of a barrel of crude oil was plummeting. Ultimately reaching the mid $20's per barrel before rebounding to the mid $30s by early March 2016 (breaching even the 2009 lows, which occurred in the middle of one of the worst economic recessions in modern history). As the OPEC nations dug their heels in to preserve market share, they refused to cut production in the faces of falling prices for the first time in years. The result was an acceleration in the collapse of crude prices that had largely been under way for eighteen months. While this development was seen as boon for consumers, as less disposable income would be needed for transportation fuels and could be used for other consumer purchases, the financial community was less sanguine. All the credit that had been extended to fuel the production boom now had much less revenue available for debt service. Defaults that had begun to escalate in late 2014 began to soar throughout 2015. The junk-bond market and banks were exposed to significant losses (the former more than the latter). The decline in prices was an energy trader's nightmare.

The energy industry, including companies both large and small, had to slash capital-spending budgets massively as the topline revenue for their business dried up. It turns out that the massive price spike of 2007–2008 was an oil company's dream, and the price collapse was conversely a managerial challenge financially. Remember that this challenge is driven by a glut of too much oil on the market as opposed to not enough. While one can certainly sympathize with any company whose revenue recedes due to a price collapse of their product, the reality is that lower energy costs are good for just about everyone else, so the author's view is that this development is an unabashed positive for the economy overall. It also bears repeating that oil as a percentage of gross domestic product (GDP) is now very low compared to what it was in 1972–1973, making wild swings in crude prices much more manageable in any macroeconomic sense. A collapse in oil prices does, however, challenge the notion that we are running out of it. But if this price collapse is wreaking havoc on large oil companies, what will the impact be for those companies who engage in hydraulic fracture? Those are typically smaller companies or start-ups. How will they fare, and what will happen to production in the face of much lower crude prices?

It is a well-known fact in the industry that the primary source of production increases in recent years comes from the nonconventional sources, such shale oil, where the new drilling techniques enable production that would not otherwise be available for use. It is also a commonly understood that tight oil from unconventional sources enabled by better technology will be a driver of increases in crude production for at least the next twenty years.[84] In the eyes of major energy authorities, the unconventional source for crude oil is not a fleeting phenomenon.

It is worth mentioning that while the IEA has now regularly acknowledged unconventional tight oil as a reliable source of crude and that it will likely be so for years, even decades, to come. This was not always the case. In 2006, shortly after so many peak-oil books had been published proclaiming the end of oil and civilization as we knew it, the IEA published a fact sheet entitled "World Energy Outlook 2006—Fact Sheet—Global Energy Trends," and it made no mention of increased production coming from unconventional sources or the use of technologies such as hydraulic fracture or horizontal drilling. Astonishingly, the 2006 Fact Sheet contained the following passage:

Oil Supply is increasingly dominated by a small number of producers. OPECs share of global supply grows significantly, from 40 percent now to 48 percent. Non-OPEC conventional crude oil output peaks in

---

84 International Energy Agency (IEA), World Energy Outlook 2013 Fact Sheet. The 2014 Fact Sheet reiterates this notional directionally, but is not as bullish as the 2013 Fact Sheet on the longevity of production increases for US unconventional oil.

the middle of the next decade [2016]. *Conventional oil accounts for the lion's share of the increase* in global supply, but non-conventional resources—mainly oil sands in Canada—play an increasingly important role (Emphasis Added).

The foregoing passage illustrates that even the IEA was assuming a peak-oil scenario, at least as far as the conventional resources are concerned, and when they get around to mentioning the nonconventional sources, it is the Canadian oil sands that are referenced. Nothing is said of American tight oil or of the budding improvements in drilling technology. When you refer to the 2006 IEA Oil Fact Sheet, it has this to say:

Oil Supply is increasingly dominated by a small number of producers. OPECs share of global supply grows significantly, from 40 percent now to 48 percent at the end of the outlook period [2030]. Saudi Arabia remains by far the largest producer. Non-OPEC conventional crude oil output peaks in the middle of the next decade [2016], though natural gas liquids continues to rise.

So for both published fact sheets, the developments in the United States' unconventional drilling space was basically not mentioned or discussed in any way at all. The IEA did not have these developments on the radar screen in a manner justifying any public discussion as recently as 2006. That means they too were late in acknowledging their impact, as unconventional production in the United States began to surge two years later, but the infrastructure to put that wherewithal in place had to be accumulated in the years prior. There is no excuse for the IEA to have omitted this discussion. This oversight by a major agency in the energy policy space does reiterate my point that just about everybody missed the shale oil development until it was undeniable and irrefutable. Few saw it coming, and fewer still predicted it would come at all. I do not mention these facts for the purpose of discrediting the IEA; conversely, I have cited their work repeatedly in writing this book. Rather I merely offer their oversight on unconventional drilling developments as an illustration of just how pervasive the idea was that we were running out of oil. Events unfolded over the ensuing decade to debunk this notion, and the literal overabundance of crude oil today proves that the peak-oil theory is just plain wrong.

Back to the question at hand: If hydraulic fracture and horizontal drilling techniques made all of this abundance possible, how likely are they to continue to yield sustainable production increases in the future? The IEA thinks US tight oil will contribute to unconventional production increases only through the mid-2020s.[85] I do not believe this is ultimately how events will shake out. Remember that the IEA was late to the fracking party. As we saw with the 2006 fact sheets and IEA Energy Outlook, they said almost nothing of these techniques, much less predicting what would transpire in ensuing

---

85 Ibid., *2014 Fact Sheet.*

years. The IEA was notably more bullish on unconventional sources of oil in their outlook published in 2013. There is no question that collapsed crude prices—brought on by too much supply—will have a chilling impact on shale-driller production. Production from hydraulic fracture in unconventional locations will surely decline in the immediate term. But this author takes the position that as supply-and-demand imbalances are ultimately worked through and prices begin to rise again, the economic incentives to harvest crude oil from these techniques will prove irresistible, and production increases will resume.

With that said, let's move on to a discussion of views of energy authorities who share my view. What better place to begin than with what the US federal government thinks of the prospects for oil production coming from unconventional sources, such as tight oil or shale oil? As of 2015, US governmental projections as noted by the US Energy Information Administration (EIA) are marked for strong growth in the domestic production of crude oil from tight formations through 2020 and then a flattening of demand for crude oil resulting in a net material decline in the importation of crude oil and other petroleum liquids.[86] Moreover, as the Annual Energy Outlook provided by the EIA is a series of forecasts based on various scenarios, it is worth mentioning that the EIA specifically asserts that under the majority of the scenarios, net energy imports to the United States,

---

86 US Energy Information Administration (EIA) Annual Energy Outlook 2015, 2.

including all fuels, decline and ultimately end by 2030 for the first time since the 1950s.[87] This point bears repeating for my peak-oil obsessed brethren: according to the US EIA, the United States will cease to be a net importer of energy for the first time since Eisenhower was president and Elvis was early in his career. Even more astonishing is the estimation by the EIA that by 2017, the United States is expected to be a net exporter of natural gas under all scenarios or "cases."[88] Remember that hydraulic fracture and horizontal drilling are just as key for the production of natural gas as they are for the harvesting of domestic crude oil. I think it is incontrovertible that the EIA scenarios acknowledge the importance of these techniques in the years to come and that they are not merely fleeting events, but rather are changing the energy mix for the United States in fundamental ways and on a permanent basis. By the published work of the US Energy Department, fracking is here to stay, as is horizontal drilling, along with the fruits of their labor—crude oil and natural gas.

Another important point to be made is the EIA view of the degree to which petroleum and other liquids will remain a relatively large component of the country's energy mix through 2040, comprising roughly 35 percent of total energy consumed.[89] Add natural gas to the mix, and the percentage rises to 62 percent of total energy consumed through 2040.[90]

---

87 Ibid.

88 Ibid.

89 Ibid., 5.

90 Ibid.

So, according to EIA scenario analysis, approximately 62 percent of all energy consumed in the nation a quarter century from now will still be sourced by oil and gas, and we will have ceased to be an energy importer by that time—all thanks to hydraulic fracture and horizontal drilling.

Keep in mind that the EIA did not even include shale gas in its 2009 Outlook, so for the agency to do an about-face on such a grand scale is quite noteworthy. Like so many other key policy makers in the industry, the EIA has gone from an onlooker peering from the outside in to a full-fledged acknowledgment that hydraulic fracture has changed the energy dynamic permanently and in fundamental ways.

We have already briefly touched on the 2014 World Energy Outlook for the International Energy Agency and have spoken to information in their 2014 fact sheets, which acknowledge a multidecade future for hydraulic fracture and horizontal drilling and that the production they enable from tight formations will contribute to crude-oil production growth for years to come. While it is not necessary to reiterate what has already been covered, it is worth noting that the two primary nonindustry authorities regarding energy policy view these technological developments as lasting and paradigm changing dynamics. Additionally we have already surveyed the point of view of major oil producing companies, and those views are aligned with the EIA and IEA.

Not surprisingly, the American Petroleum Institute (API), the primary trade advocacy organization for the oil and gas industry, is as bullish on the prospect of hydraulic fracture (fracking) and horizontal drilling as other sources we have noted. The API notes that fracking has now been used in at least one million US oil wells and has safely produced over seven billion barrels of oil and six hundred trillion cubic feet of natural gas.[91] Moreover, the API notes the following regarding the future of fracking:

> Fracking makes it possible to produce oil and natural gas in places where conventional technologies are ineffective. Access to new wells encourages economic growth and provides energy for all Americans. The oil and natural gas industry is committed to the continued safe and responsible development of our domestic resources and ensuring that the public is part of the conversation. *Informed dialogue is critical since studies estimate that up to 80 percent of natural gas wells drilled in the next decade will require hydraulic fracturing technology* (emphasis added).[92]

Clearly the view from the industry players and their trade association is that fracking has become a bedrock methodology for the production of oil and gas and will continue to be so for years to come.

A quick survey of the US Geological Service website offers a treasure trove of articles and other information discussing the technical specifications of fracking as well as data on the

---

91 American Petroleum Institute, "Energy Tomorrow," December 16, 2015, energytomorrow.org.

92 Ibid.

history and trends associated with it.[93] In January 2015, the USGS published data analysis regarding fracking trends that concluded that the hydraulic-fracture and horizontal-drilling techniques are unlocking unconventional oil and gas accumulations as well as contributing to the energy reserves of the United States.[94]

The Council on Foreign Relations (CFR) is another entity that has published an article acknowledging the durability of fracking as a force for energy production for the years to come.[95] The authors squarely address the question of how much oil and gas is harvestable via these techniques by deferring to the Energy Information Agency projections that shale gas production from tight shale formations will likely continue rising through 2040, with the usual caveats that price swings, technology, and geopolitics could alter the trajectory.[96] Suffice it to say that there is nothing in the article to suggest that peak oil is around the corner. To the contrary, the article properly notes that the shale-gas revolution unleashed by hydraulic fracture and horizontal drilling has positioned the United States to become a net exporter of natural gas with US regulators approving the construction of five Liquid

---

93 See http://energy.usgs.gov/OilGas/UnconventionalOilGas/Hydraulic Fracturing.aspx for access to USGS information regarding hydraulic fracture.

94 USGS Scientific Investigations Report 2014-5131, *Trends in Hydraulic Fracturing Distributions and Treatment Fluids, additives, Proppants, and Water Volumes Applied to Wells Drilled in the United States from 1947–2010—Data Analysis and Comparison to Literature.*

95 Council on Foreign Relations, *Hydraulic Fracturing (Fracking),* by James McBride and Mohammed Aly Sergie, Updated June 10, 2015.

96 Ibid.

Natural Gas (LNG) terminals.[97] Remember that as recently as the middle of the last decade, it was widely believed that the US domestic production of natural gas would have collapsed by now, and the prevailing questions were how to procure adequate foreign sources of natural gas and at what cost. Someone flouting the notion that the United States would be transformed into a net exporter of natural gas would have been laughed out of the room in 2006 or even 2009.

The chorus of voices extoling the virtues of shale oil and gas unlocked by hydraulic fracture and horizontal drilling is not limited to just government agencies, the oil and gas industry and its advocates, or the CFR. The Bipartisan Policy Center (BPC) recently wrote a letter to Congress, signed by its founder Jason Grumet in November, urging the lifting of the oil export ban.[98] Grumet urged the Congress to lift the ban and allow the United States to export crude oil for the first time in decades, as it would stimulate increased production and lower prices over the long run. By December, the US Congress, as part of a major bipartisan budget deal, lifted the ban on oil exports from the United States for the first time since 1975.

It should be emphatically stated that the prospect of the United States, a net oil importer for decades, becoming an oil exporter in the company of Russia and Saudi Arabia is a development made possible by fracking. Period. Without these new

---

97 Ibid.

98 Jason Grumet, President and Founder of the *Bipartisan Policy Center*. *November 20, 2015.*

drilling techniques, the oil and gas retrieved from these tight formations would still be trapped there indefinitely. To be in a position to start exporting crude oil necessarily assumes the durability of hydraulic fracture and horizontal drilling as an extraction method and that the technical specifics of these methods will continue to evolve in ways that are very likely to continue harvesting oil in ever greater quantities. If the increase in crude were viewed as a temporary phenomenon, then there would be no basis for lifting the export ban. The fact that Congress has acted to alter a policy in place for nearly half a century is the clearest possible sign there is a widespread belief that shale gas production is here to stay and will drive production increases for the foreseeable future.

The Institute for Energy Research (IER) has also weighed in on the topic of fracking and is squarely in the shale-gas-as-new-frontier camp. When the Energy Information Administration published its 2013 Annual Energy Outlook Reference Cases, the IER heralded hydraulic fracture and horizontal drilling as a transformative development with the capacity to "unlock hundreds of years of affordable energy supply under our feet."[99] The press release when on to suggest that the oil and gas production increases driven by these new technologies in shale formations on state and private lands "is nothing short of a miracle."[100]

---

99 See Institute for Energy Research at http://instituteforenergyresearch. org/press/2013–annual-energy-outlook-hydraulic-fracturing-key-to-u-s-energy-future/.
100 Ibid.

To summarize, the sharp production increases in the production of crude oil and natural gas in the United States beginning in 2008 and continuing unabated through 2015 is nothing short of a revolution, one that was enabled by advancements in technologies related to hydraulic fracture and horizontal drilling. As these technologies had their genesis in 1947, with transformational developments occurring in connection with them half a century later, it must be assumed that these technologies are amenable to further development and are likely to continue to be modified in ways that will result in production increases going forward. If fracking has its initial origins with the Truman administration and is utterly altering the energy landscape five decades later, I think its durability is self-evident. I have gone out of the way to marshal various other sources sharing this view to give credence to the fact that there is ample reason to believe fracking will be a fixture in America's energy industry for the foreseeable future and will continue to expand worldwide over time.

It would not be right to talk about the future of hydraulic fracture and horizontal drilling and the oil they release from the tight-shale formations without taking into account the view from the Organization of Petroleum Exporting Countries (OPEC). At the end of 2015, OPEC released its annual World Oil Outlook (WOO), and it was quite sobering. First, the 2015 WOO asserts that crude oil will remain central to the global energy mix for the next quarter century.[101] OPEC fully acknowledges that future supply will

---

101 OPEC, *World Oil Outlook*, 2015, 5.

increasingly come from diversified sources.[102] The most astonishing facet of the 2015 WOO is that OPEC does not project the cost of a barrel of crude oil to hit ninety-five dollars again until 2040.[103] During the first half of January 2016, a barrel of crude oil fetched thirty-one dollars in world markets. That is truly astonishing. As a point of reference, in June 2014, the price of a barrel of Brent Crude oil was $110, a level that apparently, according to OPEC, is not likely to be seen again for decades. The impact of this admission cannot be overstated. Essentially this is an acknowledgment that the nonconventional sources of crude oil have been so successful, the result of which is a massively oversupplied global market for crude that will take decades to work off given the growth in the world economy is likely to trend below potential for quite some time—in OPEC's view.

Remember that there are wild cards. Global growth could accelerate faster than anticipated and bring supply and demand back in favor of one-hundred-dollar crude sooner than what OPEC presently anticipates. With that understood, the basic dynamic of the existing situation is that the current oversupply is effectively a glut of historic proportions. This is easily on the level of the mid-1980s glut and may last as long or longer. With this backdrop, the howling predictions of peak oil that reached hurricane levels a decade ago look downright laughable.

---

102 Ibid.
103 Ibid., 8.

As a final word on the future potential for hydraulic fracture, I will defer again to Mark Mills. You will recall in chapter 1, I referenced at length an excellent work Mr. Mills published with Peter Huber in 2005 called *The Bottomless Well*. Mr. Mills recently published a detailed analysis regarding the continued rapid improvements being made to shale-extraction techniques, where he surveys developments in data analytics to improved rig productivity, robotics, and advanced materials.[104] In the report, Mills offers a perfect example of the kind of development occurring across the industry. He writes,

> Gains in rig productivity also continue to emerge, thanks to growing operational experience, the application of higher pressures, more effective chemicals, better spacing of multiple wells, more efficient motors, and better cementing and perforating of pipe. *Operators, for example, increasingly use more powerful pumps to move the water and mixture faster and at higher pressures, greatly increasing the amount of sand used to keep the shale cracks open* (emphasis added and citations omitted).[105]

This is but a single sampling of the kinds of advancements in drilling covered by Mills. His report is a detailed accounting

---

104 Mark Mills, *Shale 2.0, Technology and the Coming Big Data Revolution in America's Shale Oil Fields,* Manhattan Institute, Center for Energy Policy and the Environment (CEPE) Report No. 16. (May 2015).
105 Ibid., 5.

of many such developments, all with the cumulative impact of driving the break-even point per well lower and lower. The trend toward technological and operational improvement will continue well into the future and yield continued increases in US crude-oil production, as have been forecasted by the EIA.

The overriding thrust of Mill's report points to an industry that will use technological innovation and improved practices to adjust to lower prices and retain competitiveness by lowering the break-even points. A couple of things to keep in mind regarding Mill's arguments. A decade ago, when there was an entire gaggle of energy soothsayers forecasting the end of oil, Mills was among the voices telling that us we were headed toward an abundance of energy, including crude oil, not Malthusian scarcity. His observations were remarkably prescient. Those of his counterparts in the peak-oil crowd were proved utterly false. Bet against Mills at your peril. Policy makers are well advised to the recommendations made by Mills, and frankly voters should be holding these policy makers accountable for a realistic energy policy that is grounded in hard science, not wishful thinking and good intentions.

My own personal view is that price fluctuations with lower prices will impact shale production in the short run. I believe periods of low prices are likely to temporarily suppress shale oil and gas production in the near term from when it was trending when the price of crude was at one hundred dollars per barrel. However, I am in complete agreement with Mills that over the long run, the trend will be one of unmistakable production increases, with fracking as a primary driver. The notion of peak oil at this juncture is simply an uninformed view that utterly overlooks the long history of ingenuity and technological advancement that are the hallmarks of the global energy industry. As I've asked previously, will oil and gas production eventually peak? Over time—yes. Perhaps a *very* long time, and no one has a firm grasp on when that is likely to occur. The last fifty years have been littered with eminent minds falling for the peak-oil trap, only to have their theories ultimately not be able to withstand the test of history.

CHAPTER 4

Ever Heard of Fire Ice?

———

CHANCES ARE YOU HAVE NEVER heard of methane clathrate. If you read the introduction to this book, you got a very brief overview and understand it is a carbon-based resource where a large amount of methane is trapped within a crystal structure of water that is similar to ice. As the methane is often stored in ice crystals in ocean sediment, and the crystals burn when ignited, the material has also been referred to as "fire ice." As I briefly stated in the introduction, these "gas hydrates," as they are often called, are found in vast quantities, primarily on the ocean floor but also in other various deposit formations around the world. The US Geological Survey refers to them collectively as gas hydrates, so that is the nomenclature I will adhere to in this book. The USGS has a primer on gas hydrates on its website, which is an excellent place to start for those learning of this potential fuel source for the first time.[106] The following points are worthy of enumeration:

---

106 See http://woodshole.er.usgs.gov/project-pages/hydrates/primer.html.

1. On Earth, gas hydrates occur naturally in some marine sediments and within and beneath permafrost.
2. Estimates are that 99 percent of gas hydrates are to be found in the marine sediments.
3. Many continental shelves in the Americas, Asia, and Africa have either recovered or inferred gas-hydrate deposits.
4. The United States has these deposits on both coasts and in the Gulf of Mexico.[107]

The USGS is careful to note that while the minimum estimates of the total amount of gas hydrates equal about four thousand times the amount of natural gas consumed in the United States in a year, much of it is not concentrated enough to be a potential target for energy-resource studies.[108] Notwithstanding the disbursed nature of the resource, the USGS has commenced the USGS Gas Hydrates Project for the purpose of contributing research that may lead to gas hydrates as a potential energy source.[109] Certainly at this stage, one has to conclude that the scientific and economic feasibility of using gas hydrates as a fuel source is under development and not anywhere near to the point where it can replace natural gas; however, it is assumed that the USGS would not be engaging in full-scale research on this potential

---

107 Ibid.

108 Ibid.

109 Ibid.; See http://woodshole.er.usgs.gov/project-pages/hydrates/energy.html.

energy source if there were no real potential for harvesting the material as a new source of hydrocarbon-based energy. By the USGS's own admission, its gas-hydrate project leads many large-scale gas-hydrates resource projects.[110] Clearly there is at least some expectation on the part of USGS that there is future economic viability with this potential fuel source.

The American Petroleum Institute (API) has recently weighed in on the prospect of "natural gas hydrates" as a potential fuel sources as well. While the API did not make any definitive predictions or assertions regarding the likely point in time that gas hydrates will be available in the marketplace in large quantities, but rather the API reiterated the degree to which the gas hydrates are in abundance and the significant research efforts under way to understand this "vast" resource.[111] In addition to the abundance of these deposits, the API also notes potential benefits that may accrue from these crystals would be advances in the storage and shipping of natural gas once this resource is fully developed.[112]

Major universities have also participated in the early stages of assessing the engineering technicalities associated with gas hydrates as a potential fuel source. In 2011, the Massachusetts Institute of Technology (MIT) issued the MITEI Natural Gas Report, Supplementary Paper on Methane Hydrates. The author of the paper was Carolyn

---

110 Ibid.

111 American Petroleum Institute, 2015. See http://www.api.org/Environment-Health-and-Safety/Environmental-Performance/Innovation/natural-gas-hydrates-may-help-fuel-the-future.

112 Ibid.

Ruppel of the USGS Gas Hydrates Project, and the paper's title is *Methane Hydrates and the Future of Natural Gas.*[113] This paper starts by noting that gas hydrates have been discussed as a potential resource for decades.[114] The paper takes the clear position that while extracting natural gas from these crystal formations on a commercial scale is still years away, the fact remains that these deposits are a potentially large source of methane "and must necessarily be included in any consideration of the natural gas supply beyond two decades from now."[115]

Ruppel's paper proceeds with summarizing much of the technical background regarding the physical makeup of the hydrates, where they are to be found and estimates on quantity. There is much discussion in the article about potential harvesting methods, and the paper provides a good summary of much of the technical research done on the subject of gas hydrates dating back decades. The article notes that while commercial viability is some ways off, it concludes that "there are strong arguments to be made for a continuing R&D effort to address the remaining challenges in advancing gas hydrates along a trajectory toward viability as a resource."[116]

---

113 Carolyn Ruppel, *Methane Hydrates and the Future of Natural Gas,* Massachusetts Institute of Technology, MITEI Natural Gas Report, Supplementary Paper No. 4 on Methane Hydrates, 2011. The paper can be found at https://mitei.mit.edu/system/files/Supplementary_Paper_SP_2_4_Hydrates.pdf.

114 Ibid., 1.

115 Ibid.

116 Ibid., 15.

Perhaps most courageously, the paper takes a stab at articulating a detailed projected time line for when methane hydrates will first be commercially viable. Ruppel puts the first attempts at small-scale commercialization at between 2025 and 2030.[117] This estimate has the usual caveats that this target would be highly dependent on many factors, including the economics-of-energy prices over that period, the demand for energy, and the politics of climate change. Any one of these variables could move the end dates for commercialization around significantly. It is my position that the recent collapse in oil and gas prices will act to push the commercial viability out beyond 2030.

Ruppel's paper also discusses some of the formal estimates done on the matter that a price of $7.50 Canadian (2005 dollars) to be commercially viable, obviously much higher than today's current price. With the ongoing glut likely to take years to work off, the economic incentives for developing gas hydrates has a lessened urgency. The point is that once the day comes where natural gas prices are sustained at a level that makes the final development of gas hydrates into a large-scale fuel, that development is highly likely to occur, and all the basic R&D has either been started, is under way, or is already planned.

Furthermore when the exigency of painfully high natural gas prices eventually arrives (and it will someday), the economic viability of this resource will take a quantum leap. Also we have no way of knowing what breakthrough we will see

---

117 Ibid., 17.

with the current R&D. If there is a technical breakthrough that brings allows for large-scale extraction, storage transfer, and consumption, with the effect being to lower the break-even point in comparison with existing natural gas stores, the economic viability of this resource could arrive on the schedule Ruppel notes in her paper.

In addition to the foregoing authorities pointing to the great potential of "burning ice," the EIA also weighed in on the prospect of methane hydrates as an energy source in 2012 and noted that gas hydrates may represent one of the world's largest reservoirs of carbon-based fuel.[118] The issue with harvesting this abundant fuel source, according to the EIA, is that the abundance of existing natural gas at very low prices erases most of the economic incentive to fully develop gas hydrates for large-scale consumption.[119] In other words, there is good scientific reason to believe the resource is there, but harvesting it at the present time is not economically feasible and likely won't be well into the future. The EIA goes on to note that the estimates of the amount of gas-hydrate deposits as of 2012 were potentially as much as those of all coal and natural gas combined.[120] Again further advancements in technology and better economic conditions conducive to harvesting the resource must exist for there to be additional harvesting. Toward that end, however, the EIA did mention

---

118 Energy Information Agency, Today in Energy: *Potential of Gas Hydrates is Great, but Practical Development Is Far Off.* November 7, 2012.
119 Ibid.
120 Ibid.

that the US Department of Energy had selected fourteen gas-hydrate research projects as of YE 2012 for funding,[121] so the formal government interest in developing the resource is demonstrable. The EIA acknowledged the possibility that in the future, gas hydrates may be a potential source of natural gas.[122]

The EIA is not the only government agency to speak to the issue of gas hydrates as a future source of natural gas. The Office of Fossil Energy, which is like the EIA, is a wing of the energy department, but one that is a key driver of energy research, and has written on the issue of methane hydrates with a slightly more favorable lens. The Office of Fossil Energy (the Office) summarizes that *"the energy content of methane occurring in hydrate form is immense, possibly exceeding the combined energy content of all other known fossil fuels* (emphasis added).[123] The Office has also noted that the published Department of Energy goal is "to develop the tools and technologies to allow environmentally safe methane production from arctic and domestic off shore hydrates."[124] The web posting then goes on to list the main R&D categories supported by the DOE pertaining to gas hydrates.[125]

Clearly, the Department of energy is spending hard-earned US taxpayer dollars in gas-hydrate research and

---

121 Ibid.

122 Ibid.

123 US Department of Energy, Office of Fossil Energy. See http://energy.gov/fe/science-innovation/oil-gas-research/methane-hydrate.

124 Ibid.

125 Ibid.

development because it is a good bet. The methane is known to be contained in the crystal formation, but the technical process for extracting the methane economically and safely has not yet occurred on a commercial scale. The DOE is betting that with taxpayer money, these issues will be solved, and it is actively participating in and orchestrating research and development on the matter in concert with the USGS. It is, therefore, documentable that the US federal government, through the Departments of Energy and the Interior, is actively facilitating the development of gas hydrates as a potential, large-scale commercial source of natural gas that may be commercially viable in the 2030s. The US federal government is doing this at the same time it was a signatory in the Paris Agreement, pledging to limit global mean temperatures to no more than two degrees Celsius by 2080, which would effectively require the end of carbon-based fuels in the opinion of many experts.

The nature of the bet is, as has been said many times by many people, that natural gas is going to need to be a "bridge fuel" until renewables are 100 percent commercially viable. The development of gas hydrates will ensure that possibility, as they would add a massive quantity of natural gas reserves to an already large and growing reserve from tight-shale formations. Clearly then, natural gas in its current form and potential hydrate form will have no difficulty supporting energy consumption for decades upon decades to come. The question to be asked is what is the real time line for wind, solar, and other renewables when natural gas is available in such astounding, previously unimaginable quantities at *very* low prices. That is indeed one of the foremost energy puzzles of our day. As a society, we appear to want desperately off of fossil fuels, but we have come to find we have these energy sources in multiple times the quantities we previously thought. The price has dropped precipitously and therefore raises the competitive bar with renewables, which already start at a cost disadvantage even under the previously much higher oil and gas costs of the pre-2014 era.

Bear in mind that even before the massive price drops for oil and gas beginning in late 2014, renewables required massive subsidies from the US federal government to increase their share of the total energy mix. How much in subsidy? Congress asked the same question of the Energy Information Agency in 2014 and reported an answer that many taxpayers will, no doubt, find sobering. First some background. The EIA performed that analysis over a three-year period, including subsidies from fiscal years 2010–2013.[126] Over the course of this analysis period, the amount of federal subsidy directed to electricity generation rose from $11.7 billion to $16.1 billion, an increase of nearly 38 percent.[127] The EIA report shows that over this period, the subsidies for renewables increased to from $8.6 billion in 2010 to $13.2 billion for FY 2013.[128] Over the same period, the subsidies for fossil

---

126 US Energy Information Agency (EIA), Analysis and Projections, *Direct Federal Financial Interventions and Subsidies in Energy in Fiscal 2013*. March 23, 2012. See http://www.eia.gov/analysis/requests/subsidy for further details and analysis.

127 Ibid.

128 Ibid.

fuels declined from $4.0 billion to $3.4 billion in 2013.[129] So, as a matter of public record, the subsidies for renewables are on the rise at a rapid rate, and the subsidies for fossil fuels are declining over the same time period. Also keep in mind that these federal subsidies for renewables were in place at one-hundred-dollar-per-barrel crude. How effective would subsidies for renewables at 2013 levels be in an environment where the bottom dropped out of fossil-fuel prices? Won't there be more subsidies required for renewables in such an environment? Of course there will, which is why the subsidies continue through FYs 2015 and 2016.

This author's view is that subsidies in the multiple billions will be required for alternative sources and at twice the rate required for fossil fuels for as far as the eye can see. Such a sentiment is widely understood and acknowledged, even by those investing heavily in wind and solar energy. For example, famed investor Warren Buffet admitted that continuing to invest in wind energy is highly dependent on the continuation of the federal subsidies, bluntly telling an audience in 2014 that without the credits, there would be no reason to build the wind farms.[130] A good illustration of why is the example I note elsewhere in this book. Take the summer of 2011 in Dallas—record heat and record demand for electricity, with wind farms in the state utterly idle in the windless

---

129 Ibid.

130 Nancy Pfotenhauer, "Big Wind's Bogus Subsidy," *US News and World Report*, May 12, 2014. See http://www.usnews.com/opinion/blogs/nancy-pfotenhauer/2014/05/12/even-warren-buffet-admits-wind-energy-is-a-bad-investment.

scorching heat. In fact, wind farms are typically operated at about 30 percent of their capacity due to exactly this kind of mismatch between demand and when the wind blows.[131]

Clearly without the subsidies for renewables, companies like Berkshire Hathaway would have no reason to invest because the investment does not make economic sense on its own at the present time. It is also worth noting that the subsidies for wind and solar energy have been around for decades. I believe they will be required for several more decades before these forms are viable on their own. Frankly, that is not a net negative so long as it is understood by the tax-paying public what the lead time for these energy sources really is and that we understand that fossil fuels will need to carry the day for decades before we can reliably switch and become completely dependent on the alternative sources.

The inescapable conclusion I reach in reviewing EIA's write-up is that we know the material is there is massive quantities, but much more needs be done before it is commercially viable—more in the way of technology to harvest and a better economic environment to provide the necessary incentives to do so. If those stars line up, this may well be a long-term replacement for natural gas. I believe this is likely to occur throughout the next half a century because the hard reality is that the wind- and solar-energy prospects are far off in the future in terms of self-sustaining economic viability. Battery technology is simply not where it needs to be to make these workable at present. For example, how is electricity

---

131 Ibid.

from solar or wind to be generated at night to heat your home in the winter when the wind is not blowing? It can't be, so it needs to be generated when conditions warrant and then subsequently stored. The storage capacity is not there yet and won't be for years. These energy sources will require large amounts of government subsidies far into the future. Gas hydrates will very likely be something that is developed and viable possibly as soon as the third decade of this century. Current estimates are that renewables will comprise about 20 percent of the energy mix by 2040. As this book has already pointed out, natural gas and oil will be more than 60 percent of the mix well into the second half of this century. Shale gas and the development of gas hydrates will ensure there is harvestable natural gas for an extensive period. If the gas hydrates plan pans out as evidence suggests, then natural gas is a reliable resource for the rest of this century and beyond, and it will be positioned to accommodate significant growth in global economic output.

There is no question in my mind that mankind will ultimately harvest the sun's energy directly as well as that from wind and flowing rivers, and carbon-based energy will wane into the history books. My own personal inclination is that 2080 is about as viable a date as Al Gore's desire to be rid of the internal combustion engine by 2020. I believe that when we finally get to 2080, liquid fuels (either refined from crude oil or some new kind of liquefied natural-gas engine) will power most of our transportation. Getting battery technology to where it needs to be to allow an electric motor to truly compete with an internal combustion engine as an alternative for automotive transportation is going to require some breakthroughs.

Let me present a few facts to consider. At the present time, battery technology in cars like the Chevy Volts, Nissan Leafs, Fisker Karmas, and Teslas allow for about one hundred miles' worth of driving, whereas a tank of gas can get an internal combustion engine twice that distance on a V6 engine and really fuel-efficient four-cylinder engines can easily get three hundred miles. An electric car with a need to recharge every one hundred miles, which is a significantly longer process than filling up the tank, is really not all that competitive. Perhaps that explains why truly electric cars and hybrids only sell a few thousand units per year. For those who do not already know, the US market alone is typically fifteen million cars and light trucks per year. It will be a big deal when electric and hybrid car sales reach even 1 percent of that market (150,000 vehicles), and that is not expected until close to 2020. There are definitely improvements in battery technology in the pipeline, but many of these are still in the development phase. To be sure, the technology gradually improves for the rest of this decade and modest breakthroughs occur after 2020, but some of the really promising technologies that could allow an electric car to go, say, four hundred miles before needing to be recharged, are more than a decade away.

Then there is the whole other question of how to build infrastructure to put charging stations in place on the same scale as gas stations are. After all, it is the ubiquity of fueling stations that makes auto transport so viable. You can get a fill-up pretty much anywhere unless you are driving through the Mojave or Utah deserts. It will be a long time before you can take a two-or-three-day road trip in an electric car with the same piece of mind regarding your ability to recharge on a comparable level to what you can do in a car powered by liquid fuels. I fully stipulate that one day, we will all be driving around our electric cars, even on the road trips, and the internal combustion engine will fade away into history's sunset. I am just extremely skeptical that this will occur before 2080 without massive breakthroughs from technological ideas that are, at present, basically on the drafting board.

CHAPTER 5

Is the Recent Technological Breakthrough in the Petroleum Industry Replicated in Any Other Commodity Businesses?

———

IF READERS ASSUME THAT BY my phrasing the title of this chapter in the form of a question that I mean it to be a rhetorical question—one for which I have an answer in mind—they would be correct. I do believe that what we just saw over the past ten years in connection with oil and gas going from scarcity to abundance via technological innovation is a story that has applicability to a broad range of commodities. That will be the subject of this chapter. Recall that in the introduction, I referenced the limits-to-growth line of thinking of decades past that every now and then makes its way back into public discourse; it did in the middle of the last decade on a number of fronts, including the peak-oil salesmen. The projections made in the early 1970s were that there would be widespread, chronic shortages of key raw materials required for the industrial age by the turn of the century. You can be sure this line of thinking will resurface every time there is a price spike in commodities and energy.

When these doomsday diatribes are written, very little is said about pending technological advancements that may act to alter their projections. In fact, these alarmists typically do not even see or fully understand these innovations, which is why they remain silent to them. That so many of the peak-oil doomsayers didn't even mention fracking or horizontal drilling is case in point.

At the end of 2015, the middle of the current decade, the state of all commodities including industrial commodities can be aptly summed up by the World Bank as follows: "Ample supplies and weak demand, especially for industrial commodities, contributed to the continued slide in most commodity prices in the third quarter of 2015."[132] In the same document, the World Bank goes on to say, "All main commodity price indices are expected to decline in 2015, *mainly owing to ample supply*, and in the case of industrial commodities, slowing demand in China and emerging markets" (emphasis added).[133] So forty-plus years after the Club of Rome told us we were all going to be mired in some neo-Malthusian nightmare of famine and depravity, one of our most acute problems in the short term is price weakness due to oversupply and soft aggregate demand. We find ourselves in precisely the opposite circumstances than what the limits to growth doomsayers prognosticated a generation ago.

---

132 World Bank, *Commodity Markets Outlook-Executive Summary,* October 2015, 3.

133 Ibid.

It is hard to predict what the outlook for commodities will be decades from now because it is hard to know exactly how fast the world economy will grow, but grow it will. Commodities will be at the epicenter of such growth and will be plentiful for the most part. This book asserts that human ingenuity will always play a significant role in procuring the things we need, including commodities. New techniques and methods will develop more quickly in times of relative scarcity because necessity is the mother of invention, as the saying goes. Recall that in World War II, when the Japanese cut off the supply of natural rubber to the United States when they rolled through the South Pacific, the United States responded by quickly developing a synthetic rubber for tires and, to this day, has never looked back. This is a perfect illustration of scarcity being completely neutralized by innovation and ingenuity. It is the position of this book that the incentives for mining companies, food harvesters, farmers, and other economic actors in the supply chain for producing commodities have such powerful incentives to keep production alive (like their livelihoods) that we are not likely to have to contend with chronic shortages as a matter of course in the twenty-first century. In those instances where a severe and intractable shortage materializes, either alternative sources will ultimately be procured, thus alleviating the shortage, or the commodity will be replaced with something else as an industrial material. Just as coal replaced firewood, commodity usage is a dynamic affair.

It is also instructive that the 2015 International Monetary Fund (IMF) World Economic Outlook focused on the theme of "Adjusting to Lower Commodity Prices."[134] The IMF's take on the commodity situation as of 2015 notes that non-fuel commodity prices are under the same price pressure, as is the case with oil, and for similar reasons.[135] The primary dynamic of recent years is that high prices over the past decade led to a buildup of supply capacity that has come online at exactly the time demand has begun to slow.[136] Without getting into the arcane economic fundamentals of all the inner workings of the supply-and-demand particulars in the global marketplace, both the World Bank and IMF reports point to the fact that there is simply too much of a supply of basic commodities of all types in relation to the global demand. That is the *per se* definition of a glut, and a glut, in turn, is the diametric opposite of shortage. The various commodity producers around the world have become so adept at generating their raw materials that they have provided more than what the world can consume given present demand, and the price is collapsing—exactly opposite of what the limits-to-growth crowd predicted when I was growing up.

Other noteworthy analysts have recently opined that the supply-and-demand dynamics have acted to soften the price of most commodities, especially oil and gas, along with other industrial commodities. In September 2015, Barrons.com ran with an article from a BlackRock lead strategist,

---

134 International Monetary Fund, World Economic Outlook, "Adjusting to Lower Commodity Prices," October 2015.

135 Ibid., 5–6.

136 Ibid.

Russ Koesterich, covering the outlook for oil and other commodities. The analysis by Koesterich was hardly bullish on the near-term future of commodity prices.[137] Koesterich had the following notable quotes from his commodity overview: regarding the impact of supply on commodity prices, he writes,

> Unfortunately for investors in commodities, *over the past several years most commodities have been getting less scarce*, at least relative to demand. Commodity prices have generally been heading lower for more than four years. Based on the Bloomberg Commodity Index, the asset class is now down roughly 50 percent from its 2001 high (emphasis added).[138]

This passage reflects a stunning development. Koesterich is modest when he casually notes that "commodities have been getting less scarce." In fact, commodities of all types have become so abundant that robust levels of economic growth are required around the world in order to put any kind of floor under commodity prices. Since the time the limits-to-growth movement took off in the early 1970s, India and China have become economic powerhouses, as have many other countries in Asia. The US population has grown from 200 million to 320 million, and the world population is now

---

137 Russ Koesterich, *BlackRock's Outlook for Oil and Other Commodities,* posted on Barrens.com September 30, 2015. For those who do not know, BlackRock is a leading Wall Street investment management firm.
138 Ibid.

over 7 billion; yet we have so many stores of commodities across the board that prices have collapsed, as reflected by the 50 percent decline in the Bloomberg Commodities Index in four years. Koesterich goes on to say,

> Apart from slower growth, lower inflation and a stronger dollar, excess supply in many commodities is contributing to the drop in prices. This is evident when you look at global trade numbers. Many have pointed out that global trade is slowing, a trend that has a disproportionate impact on many emerging markets. *What is less remarked on is that volume remains relatively steady. Instead, most of the drop has been driven by lower prices, a sign of excess supply* (emphasis added).[139]

Again forty-plus years from the Club of Rome doomsday predictions, there is so much abundance with commodities that prices have collapsed at even modest economic growth occurring globally. We have not been in a worldwide recession in the past four years, yet commodity prices have declined by half. This is not the stuff of shortage or Malthusian desperation. China and India have lifted hundreds of millions of people out of poverty—and still we have so much commodity abundance that the price has imploded (that is unless one were to view a 50 percent decline in prices as somehow "moderate").

---

139 Ibid.

A look at individual commodities is illustrative. Take copper as an example because it is a bedrock material for industrialized life and is an especially good conductor of electricity. Therefore, it is indispensable in most electronic and electrical products. At present, the US Geological Survey estimates that there are some 700 million tonnes (Mt) of copper reserves worldwide.[140] As worldwide copper mining production is typically about 18.7 Mt annually,[141] there is enough known reserves at the present time to support 37.5 years of copper mining production at current rates. Moreover, there is a deposit category called "identified copper resources," which defines a resource whose grade, quality, and quantity are known or estimated from specific geological evidence.[142] By that definition, the global copper deposits are 100 Mt (or 2.1 billion tonnes),[143] which is a deposit base that would support current global copper production from mining activity for another 113 years. There is yet another deposit category referred to as "undiscovered copper resources," which is where the existence of the copper resource is only postulated or are mixed in with deposits of such grade and physical location so as to render their extraction infeasible economically.[144]

---

140 US Geological Survey, *Mineral Commodity Summaries.* January 2015, 2. The copper summary can be found at http://minerals.usgs.gov/minerals/pubs/commodity/copper/mcs-2015–coppe.pdf.

141 Ibid.

142 International Copper Study Group, *The World Copper Fact Book 2015*, 7.

143 Ibid.

144 Ibid.

Estimates are 3,500 Mt (3.5 billon tonnes) of undiscovered copper resources globally,[145] which would support 187 years of mining production at current levels.

When you add up identified and undiscovered resources, the total is 5,600 Mt of total copper resources,[146] which would support about 300 years' worth of current copper-mining production rates. So to summarize, there is roughly thirty-eight years' worth of proven reserves at current mining production rates, which is a sure bet. Then there is an additional 113 years' worth of production if you focus on the identified copper resources, which is a very good bet. Add on top of that the 187 years' worth of production in the fuzzier bet that is the undiscovered copper resources, and when you them both up for the total resources, you have deposits covering about 300 years' worth of copper at today's production rates on top of known reserves. Then comes the whopper: add the known reserves to the total resources, and the number is 6,300 Mt (6.3 billion tonnes of copper deposits).[147] Think about that for a moment. There is 338 years' worth of copper at current global mining production rates.

A main tenant of modern economic theory in connection with commodity extraction is that if there is another price spike down the road, all the undiscovered copper resources that are known to be in various locations but are not economically or profitably retrievable at current prices with current

---

145 Ibid.
146 Ibid.
147 Ibid.

technologies will become economical at higher prices. Also assume that technology will advance to take advantage of those higher prices. If there is money to be made in getting at the copper, rest assured that the copper will be extracted. With what we know about today's geological evidence and technologies, there is a generation's worth of copper that is in the category of known reserves and will support production through 2055 at today's mining rates. For basically the rest of a middle-aged adult's life from this moment on, current copper mining production rates are supportable for the rest of that adult's life. When you start factoring in the other deposit categories, there are copper resources for many, many lifetimes. As I have shown, there are enough worldwide copper deposits to cover today's production rates for a period longer than the United States has even formally been a country.

The key similarities copper has with crude oil is that there is a large base of what is referred to, as I've noted before, technically recoverable material, but it cannot be classified as a formal reserve for accounting purposes because there are questions about the economic viability of extracting the material at today's price and with today's technology. As we have seen in recent years with crude oil, both of these variables can change materially in a short amount of time. The core economic tenant is that when the price incentive is great enough to justify enhancing existing technologies with new investment, that new investment will occur and be deployed, adding capacity to the output of the material and changing it from technically recoverable to a known reserve. This cycle happens with all commodities and will continue to happen with all commodities for generations to come. There simply is not an economic basis for the scarcity over the long run. As has been asserted in this book repeatedly, human ingenuity will not stand for it. The survival instinct is too strong. We humans are hardwired to go after and procure the things we need or die trying. There are too many examples of scarcity being turned into abundance. Crude oil and copper are merely the most recent.

In order to drive home the point, we will survey another example using gold, which has become an important commercial resource and a core material for a modern economy. The USGS estimates there are 54,000 tonnes of gold in reserves worldwide.[148] The World Gold Council puts the figure at 32,686 tonnes in reserve as of December 2015.[149] The Council's published views on the matter of gold supply is that it has become diverse, and the companies that mine for it are investing in new technologies, processes, and explorations to support the ongoing demand for gold.[150] Gold has become a strategic resource, with uses now far exceeding jewelry and fine, finished artifacts. It is used in nanotechnology space and is a key ingredient in computer technology, so much so that the USGS once wrote in the early 2000s

---

148 US Geological Survey, *Mineral Commodity Summaries,* February 2014. See the following posting: http://minerals.usgs.gov/minerals/pubs/commodity/gold/mcs-2014-gold.pdf.

149 World Gold Council, *Latest Official World Gold Reserves,* December 9, 2015. See http://www.gold.org/research/latest-world-official-rgold-reserves.

150 Ibid. See supply web page at http://www.gold.org/supply-and-demand/supply.

that obsolete computers contained significant amounts of recoverable materials, including gold.[151] For example, there is more gold in a metric tonne of electronic scrap from personal computers than that recovered from seventeen tonnes of gold ore.[152] USGS notes, for example, that "in 1998, the amount of gold recovered from electronic scrap in the United States was equivalent to that recovered from more than 2 million metric tonnes of gold ore and waste."[153]

Clearly gold has become essential to our high-tech, electronic lifestyle; fortunately, we have a lot of it. While gold still has relative rarity, the marketplace has deemed we have sufficient amounts of what we need, as the price for gold had collapsed at the end of 2015, along with most other commodities—a development that would simply not be the case were we in a situation where gold was in chronic shortage. In late December 2015, CNBC ran with the following: "Technician: As Clouds Gather, A 'Perfect Storm' Brews For Gold."[154] In the article, Re-Essa Buckels notes that gold prices have collapsed to multiyear lows, even after years of ultra-loose, central-bank, easy-money monetary policy around the world.[155] She cites Rich Ross of Evercore ISI, who summarizes the obvious fact that gold has tracked downward in price,

---

151 US Geological Survey Fact Sheet FS-060-01, *Obsolete Computers, "Gold Mine," or High Tech Trash? Resource Recovery from Recycling.* July 2001.

152 Ibid.

153 Ibid.

154 See http://www.cnbc.com/2015/12/18/gold-has-a-perfect-storm-brewing-analyst.html.

155 Ibid.

along with other major commodities, and attributes it to the increasing strength in the US dollar and the federal rate hikes that began in December 2015. As gold prices descended toward $1,000 per ounce for the first time in many years, ask yourself whether that would be occurring if gold were scarce. Already noted is that gold is a key industrial ingredient used in computers and other electronic gear. We have been amid a technology boom that has been under way for years, so the demand for gold as a component is as good as it gets, yet there is no shortage. We can all agree that gold is a rare, precious metal, but it is not "scarce" in economic terms, and its price is reflected accordingly. Harken back to the World Gold Council comments noted above: gold miners are investing heavily in new technologies and processes to ensure that the world's gold demand is met.

Indeed that is a theme for all commodities, as is demonstrated by the sharp decline of the Bloomberg Commodity Index (BCOM), which as of December 18, 2015, reached 77.45, a more than 50 percent decline from the 158.89 value in December 2010. Specifically, there were some commodities that were hit especially hard, such as aluminum, copper, and platinum, all down comfortably in the double digits. The inescapable conclusion is that crude oil as a commodity has performed similarly to other commodities in the marketplace. There was once a time where commodities were viewed as imminently finite to the point where the sustainability of modern life was called into question, as referenced in the introduction to this book and its first chapter. But a thorough review of historical trends and current facts yields a diametrically opposite conclusion. A friend of mine once told me, "The world is a rich place," and went on to point out that wealth creation is often a political problem as much as an economic and business one. His point is well taken as we move through the middle part of this century's second decade. At the present time, key natural resource commodities and fuels are in such abundant supply that their prices have adjusted sharply downward to reflect the glut-like conditions. And as noted, this is occurring despite one of the most pronounced expansions of global economic growth, where massive new entrants into the world marketplace, such as India and China, have skewed demand for commodities massively upward. Not only did the world's commodity producers meet the demand, they exceeded it to the point where the prices cannot hold. Over the past forty-plus years, there simply were no limits to growth based on natural resource and fuel scarcity, as was predicted by some academic quarters at the time.

None of this is to say, of course, that there will never be shortages or scarcity again, as there will always be periodic moments in economic history where demand will outstrip current supply and cause a significant price surge. The point is that those instances are rarely a permanent phenomenon. Higher prices nearly always act as a catalyst for innovation, as the economic rationale for investment proves irresistible. The price of oil hit $147 dollars for a barrel of crude, and suddenly, we had more crude than we know what do so with. Over time, the general principles of macroeconomics will generally support adequate supplies of finite resources at affordable prices. Technological innovation is the one constant that can be counted on in an ever-changing global economy. Doomsday predictions of depletion need to be taken with an abundance of skepticism. Policy decisions based on faulty notions of market imperfection lead to boondoggles like the government-guaranteed financing for a crackpot business venture like Solyndra.

Government policy is better focused on soundly regulating known markets and searching for incentives to invest in new technologies. I honestly believe that was what the Obama administration was trying to do with Solyndra, but therein lies the problem. Government support for research and development should not leech into providing any kind of financial assistance for the private marketplace, other than tax incentives. Providing loan guarantees and other financial incentives starts to have the look and feel of the government attempting to play the role of venture capitalist, a role it has no business assuming and frankly a role it has no track record of success in. Moreover, there are the optics of the government picking winners and losers when it protrudes itself into the market with incentives like the ones afforded Solyndra.

In a remarkable turn of events over the past nearly half a century, lack of aggregate demand, as opposed to scarcity, is turning out to be a much bigger problem for all natural resources, including oil and gas, than the inflationary shortages of the 1970s. For those who've been around for a few decades, the shortages and price spikes of the 1970s seem like a lifetime ago—and they were (albeit a short lifetime). Since the mid-1980s, while there have been periodic price spikes in various commodities, including oil and gas, the general trend has been downward. The spikes are now the anomaly, and either stability or generally low prices are much more the norm. The price behavior is a very adequate reflection of abundance. Even the price surges for commodities from the early 2000s through 2011–2012 were short lived. Technology and industrial capacity quickly caught up with demand stoked by growth in India and China. Shortages will have to wait.

CHAPTER 6

What Is the Outlook of Carbon-Based Energy (Oil and Gas) for the Remainder of the Twenty-First Century—Will We Live in Permanent Scarcity, Abundance, or Something in Between?

———

ANY DISCUSSION OF THE FUTURE prospects for the production of oil and gas should begin with an assessment of where things stand in terms of proven reserves. This topic was briefly touched on in chapter 1, and we will pick up where we left off. As 2015 came to a close, the United States sat on the highest levels of proved reserves for natural gas in its history and the highest proved reserves for crude oil since 1972.[156]

---

156 US Energy Information Agency at http://www.eia.gov/todayinenergy/detail.cfm?id=23932 November 30, 2015.

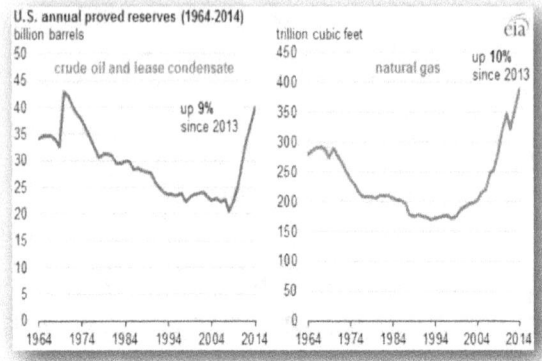

Proved reserves are volumes of oil and natural gas that geologic and engineering data demonstrate with reasonable certainty to be recoverable under existing economic and operating conditions. Clearly, the technological advancements of hydraulic fracture and horizontal drilling have contributed to the expansion of known proved reserves for oil and gas, as they have completely altered the operating-conditions portion of the equation. The upward trend of proved reserves in recent years follows almost exactly the same trends for the production increases for oil and gas.[157]

---

157 The EIA is careful to note as follows regarding the potential mobility of "proved reserves": "Because they depend on economic factors, *proved reserves shrink or grow as commodity prices and extraction costs change.* EIA's estimates of proved reserves are based on an annual survey of domestic oil and natural gas well operators" (emphasis added), Ibid. The practical impact of the way in which "proved reserves" are tabulated is that they will change over time, as commodity prices and extraction costs change. The commodity-price collapse, including crude oil, over the past two years means that it is quite foreseeable that the proved-reserve level will decline in the short run, perhaps sharply, but the oil and gas are still in the ground and can be verified by imaging and other technologies. Over the long run, however, supply-and-demand

As it stands, then, a decade and a half into the twenty-first century, the United States sits on the largest base of proved reserves for oil and gas in decades, and there is a very real possibility that, at least with respect to natural gas, the proved reserves will set records for years to come. Crude-oil reserves are also expected to continue to rise. There is simply no merit to the peak-oil claim, and truthfully, there wasn't back in 2005–2006, the apex of the peak-oil hysteria. Clearly, we started the early portion of this century in the abundance category, with all the good (low gas prices) and bad (destruction of industry profits) that entails.

There is also no merit to the notion that the United States holds a mere 2 percent of the world's oil reserves. In early 2013, in typical fashion for the current administration, the president asserted this statistic as fact in an effort to play up his administration's alternative-energy policy by scaremongering US fossil-fuel scarcity. As one can see from the chart depicted previously, crude oil and natural gas proved reserves increased by 10 percent since the president made the 2 percent assertion—a good reminder that the tabulation of proved reserves is not a static exercise but a very dynamic one. Bear in mind that there are other accounting definitions regarding oil and gas deposits, such as those that are technically recoverable but, for various reasons, are not open to extraction for regulatory reasons (e.g., the Alaskan National Wildlife Refuge, or ANWR, ore

---

dynamics will work to bring upward pressure on commodity prices, and technological innovation will continue to drive down extraction costs. Taken together, these factors will act to maintain proved reserves over time.

deposits on federal lands). At the same time the president made this assertion, the US Energy Information Administration had just issued an Annual Energy Review in September 2012 that asserted there were 220.2 billion barrels of technically recoverable oil in the United States, not that far from the proved reserves of major OPEC members.[158] Additionally, in the same report, the EIA reported there was 2,203.3 trillion cubic feet of technically recoverable natural gas in the United States.[159]

A careful analysis of reserve data released by the EIA from 1980 through 2010 reveals a steady reserve base in the face of cumulative production that far exceeds the original reserve base, indicating consistent crude-oil replenishment. From 1980 to 2010, the United States produced 77.8 billion barrels of oil and still had 20.7 billion barrels of crude in proved reserve by 2010.[160] Additionally, as the EIA proved, reserve estimate for 1980 was 31.3 billion barrels, and the production of 77.8 billion barrels of crude from 1980 to 2010 means that the United States produced 2.5 times the base reserve estimate over the ensuing thirty years.[161] Let's assume for argumentative purposes that the 1980–2010 production trend repeats itself. As the current proved reserve estimate for US crude oil is now 40 billion barrels, to produce 2.5 times the base-reserve rate through 2045 would mean the United States is on track to produce 100 billion barrels of crude oil

---

158 US EIA, *Annual Energy Review,* Table 4.1, Released September 27, 2012.

159 Ibid.

160 See Institute for Energy Research, "Exposing the 2 Percent Oil Reserves Myth, February 17, 2013, www.instituteforenergyresearch.org.

161 Ibid.

over that time, or 3.33 billion barrels of oil per year, or 9.132 million barrels per day for the next thirty years. For those not old enough to remember, US production peaked at almost ten million barrels per day in 1970, yet we stand to average that rate or higher for the next thirty years. We were supposed to be out of oil by now or on the downhill slope of the peak-oil curve, but we find ourselves revisiting production levels not seen for four decades. Indeed, EIA data depicting consistent crude-oil replenishment is but one of the many inconvenient facts for the peak-oil alarmist. The undeniable fact is that the United States is sitting on one of the world's great stores of oil and gas, whether the environmental lobby likes it or not.

Moreover, whether the environmentalist appreciates it or not, the global economy is expected to continue to grow throughout the decades to come, and that will necessitate increased energy usage. The basic theme of this chapter is that given the political toxicity associated with the use of nuclear power as a key energy source to meet growing demand and the extremely limited base that renewables are starting from as a percentage of the total energy mix, the heavy lifting for the world's energy supply will have to come from traditional sources probably for the rest of my lifetime and well into my children's adulthood. The Paris Agreement would have us weaned from carbon-based energy by 2080. Good luck with that. Remember when Al Gore published *Earth in the Balance* in the early 1990s and advocated and predicted the end of the internal combustion engine by 2020? Well, that is four short years away as of the writing of this book. Do you really believe the internal combustion engine will be gone by the end of the next president's first term? Perhaps we should be careful with wishful thinking from the alternative-energy advocates and stick with the proven information.

We will explore the nuclear-power option first. As anyone who has followed energy policy for a number of years will know, it is commonly understood that the environmental lobby has been and is likely to continue to be a loud critic of nuclear power as an energy option. The environmental lobby has been so successful in their antinuclear advocacy that there has not been a single nuclear power plant started in the United States since the Three-Mile Island incident in Pennsylvania in 1979.[162] In February 2010, President Obama announced that his administration approved an $8.3 billion loan guarantee to build the first nuclear power plant in thirty years. The environmental lobby surely must have learned in the interim three decades that stifling the development of nuclear power did not stop the economy and the demand for electricity from growing consistently. All that was accomplished by snuffing out the nuclear-power option for thirty years is the assurance that fossil fuels would be relied upon more than ever to meet energy demands, something the Obama administration clearly observed in moving forward to facilitate the construction of the first nuclear facility in a generation.

A more reasoned view of nuclear power as an energy option comes from, not surprisingly, the Massachusetts Institute of

---

162 According to treehugger.com, the last two nuclear power plants to be completed in the United States were the Watts Bar Plant in Rhea County Tennessee, whose construction commenced in 1973, completed in 1990, and came online in 1996. The second was Louisiana's River Bend Plant, which was completed in 1986.

Technology (MIT), where they have recently published a study titled *The Future of Nuclear Power*, which articulates a much more rational view of nuclear power as a legitimate source of electricity. In this study, the institution first outlines the context for the study by noting that, as I have touched on in the foreword to this book, nuclear power is an obvious alternative to fossil fuels and would, in fact, result in drastically lowering greenhouse-gas emissions were it embraced on a broad scale.[163] This study, written in proximity with the peak-oil alarmist work of 2005, reached the conclusion that at that time, nuclear power faced "stagnation and decline." Indeed, the forecasts for the energy mix out to 2030 and beyond have nuclear power as a small fraction of total global energy supply. The MIT study noted that as of 2002, nuclear power only provided 20 percent of electricity consumption in the United States.[164] The study noted that official forecasts were for a mere 5 percent increase in nuclear-power-generating capacity worldwide from 2002 to 2020, while electricity usage might grow as much as 75 percent over the same period.[165] The study advocated that nuclear energy should remain a legitimate policy option for the supply of energy as a low-carbon energy source.[166] Unfortunately, the MIT faculty recognized that the American public won't likely embrace nuclear-power expansion without substantial improvements in cost and technology.[167] This con-

---

163 Interdisciplinary MIT Study, *The Future of Nuclear Power,* Massachusetts Institute of Technology 2003, ix.

164 Ibid., 1.

165 Ibid., 1–2.

166 Ibid.

167 Ibid., 6.

clusion was reached after analysis of a scientific survey MIT itself conducted of 1,350 adults in the United States regarding their attitudes about energy in general and specifically nuclear power. The sobering reality is that over a decade ago, the public would not support large-scale expansion of nuclear energy, and there is little evidence that attitude has changed.

The unfortunate reality as of YE 2013 is that nuclear power accounts for a mere 11 percent of global electricity generation, down from a peak of 18 percent in the mid-1990s.[168] There is the prospect that policy changes will result in a global share of 12 percent for nuclear power generated electricity by 2040.[169] This means that by midcentury, the global share of electricity produced from nuclear-power generating plants is still materially below where it was at the time of Bill Clinton's reelection in 1996—all the while, electricity usage worldwide will surely have increased by some 40 percent from where it is now. Clearly, nuclear power is not poised to replace fossil fuels anytime in the foreseeable future. A significant opportunity to embrace a fuel source that would substantially contribute to the reduction of greenhouse gases will likely continue to stagnate and stall in the years to come, even in the face of surging global energy demand. Fossil fuels will carry the heavy weight for the foreseeable future until renewables become viable.

With the nuclear-power option effectively taken from the table, the pressure on other fuel sources to meet present

168 International Energy Agency, *World Energy Outlook 2014 Fact Sheet for Nuclear Power.*
169 Ibid.

demand will ensure that the intrinsic need for coal- and gas- powered electricity and petroleum-powered locomotion remains intact, at least until midcentury. At the moment, in the middle of the second decade of the twenty-first century, oil and gas are at record levels for reserves, and the United States has become the third-largest producer of crude oil, nearing the 1970 production levels by exceeding nine million barrels per day. Certainly attempting to predict the future can be a fool's errand, but a clear-eyed review of the data available today yields the conclusion that we are likely to experience abundance for the time being, and there is the clear potential for abundance for decades to come. The notions of oil scarcity as outlined by the peak-oil alarmists of a decade ago have been clearly discredited. Public policy should wholeheartedly embrace oil and natural gas as bridge fuels for the purpose of gradually replacing coal until solar and wind energy become viable (defined as competing in the marketplace without the need for continued government subsidy in either production or research and development).

As noted earlier in this chapter, there is a rational basis to estimate US crude-oil production to average over nine million barrels per day through 2045, allowing for a lengthy bridge period to the desired end state for alternative energy. The key to remember is that this production level will be an *average*, implying production may well fall below it for a time and will likely exceed it at other times. If recent history is any guide, various production rates will be driven by the price per barrel and demand. At present, we know there is a massive glut of crude on world markets, and we know current economic growth levels are not sufficient to rapidly draw down these stockpiles. It is rapidly becoming a widely held belief that the current glut will take years to work off, and prices will be depressed for an extended period as a result.

But we also know in economics that the current state never lasts indefinitely. Current trends nearly always alter over time. This glut will be no different. The only questions will be these: When does economic growth power ahead with enough inertia to draw down the stockpile, and when will production wane enough to stop adding to it? When that day comes and there is more of an equilibrium between supply and demand, the price per barrel will surely rise and may again exceed one hundred dollars per barrel. Pinning down that exact day will be difficult and will be driven by a multiplicity of variables and factors. We saw how inept the peak-oil predictions were; I will not make the same mistake. I will, however, offer what I believe to be a plausible scenario based on what happened in the first decade of this century.

Let's assume that the size and magnitude of the current glut, stacked against lackluster growth, is not fully resolved until well into the next decade. We've seen some analysts, including OPEC, predict that the current glut will last well into the 2030s, but that, in my view, assumes very modest growth in the global economy, which could easily be a variable subject to significant potential deviation. There is no reason the world economy can't accelerate significantly from its recent trends. I assume that it will ultimately do so as emerging markets continue to advance their economies and bring an ever-increasing number of consumers into the global economy, driving growth higher. It is not unreasonable to anticipate that the current glut will be worked off by the late 2020s or even sooner. When prices do again breach the one-hundred-dollar-per-barrel mark, we have the first decade of this century to offer a reasonably clear guide on what to expect in terms of production trends when that happens.

The graph immediately below, generated by the US Energy Information Administration, is very instructive in showing the uptick in prices that will follow a sustained rise in the price of oil. Remember that the price for a barrel of crude surged in 2008 to over $145 per barrel and then dropped as the world economy fell into recession. But it quickly rebounded to go back over one hundred dollars per barrel when global economic output recovered. The production from 2008 to 2015 is noted as follows:

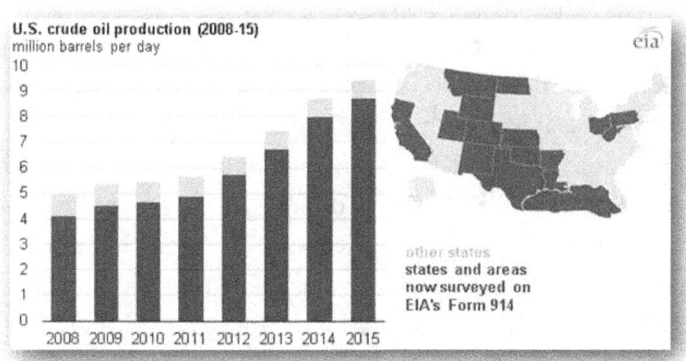

Source: US Energy Information Administration,
Monthly Crude Oil and Natural Gas Production

Note: This chart includes lease condensate. Data for 2015 reflect January through June. The EIA-914 survey began collecting monthly data in January 2015.

As we can see from this useful chart, production began to increase almost immediately after the price surge of 2008 and held steady even in the price collapse of 2009. Once one-hundred-dollar-per-barrel crude was sustained, US production took off, largely driven by the shale boom. As you can see, the lag is about five years. So if that trend repeats itself the next time we have a surge in the price per barrel of crude, then the likely outcome is a large production increase following a sustained price surge in the span of about five years. If we have a surge in the price per barrel in the late 2020s as the current glut is worked off, say by 2028, then within roughly five years we would expect to see a step-function increase in production levels, just as we did beginning in 2012, which was five years after the first surge of 2008. That would mean that beginning in the early 2030s, a massive increase in production would begin, lasting for years.

Indeed, my estimates of US crude production averaging in excess of nine million barrels per day may well see periods where it is significantly less than that as the current glut is worked off, but there is also the possibility of US production exceeding ten million barrels per day in the aftermath of the current glut. Depending on demand in the global market by the early 2030s, there is no reason production couldn't hit the EIA's most optimistic scenarios of fourteen million barrels per day in the mid-2030s. Remember that as the EIA chart indicates, the last major price spike caused US production to nearly double from 2008 to 2015. An increase to fourteen million barrels per day with the right price incentives and stacked against robust global economic growth could easily drive further massive increases in US oil production. For all the peak oilers reading this and scoffing, just remember how bad your doomsday prognostications turned out before dismissing mine. Take a good hard look at the EIA chart and reflect on it a bit. It absolutely supports the assertions I have made throughout this book. Economics 101 tells us that a sustained price increase will add economic business incentives to procure more of whatever it is that is fetching a high price. The opportunity to "strike it rich" is an age-old and powerful urge, and it will most certainly continue to work to add supply. We know where the oil is, and we are improving the techniques to extract it every year. Bet on increasing supply through the middle part of this century. If we wind up leaving crude before then, it will not be due to economics—it will be driven by other policy considerations.

However, regarding alternative sources to fossil fuels, in the end, we need to be honest with ourselves. At the present moment, wind and solar energy are clearly not viable on the same mass scale that oil, gas, and coal are. This book already touched on the problems with renewables replacing gasoline and diesel fuel as an energy source for transportation. The battery technology is simply not there, and it will take quite some time to reliably hold a charge long enough to compete with liquid fuels. As for replacing coal, renewables simply cannot compete with natural gas at the current moment. A perfect illustration of why can be found by looking back at the summer of 2011. I lived in Dallas, Texas, during that scorcher, and I remember the experience as one of the hottest summers I've ever had to bear—and it was one for the record books. There were days on end of over one hundred degrees Fahrenheit. The entire time, massive amounts of electricity were needed to run air-conditioning units, the wind farms in other areas of the state sat utterly idle due to a lack of wind to spin the turbines, and had it not been for coal and natural gas, we would have roasted for months. There is not the infrastructure in place at this time for wind and solar to replace coal as there is with natural gas. The cost of solar and wind is still massively distorted with government subsidies. Remove the subsidies, and renewables are not even worthy of discussion. As I've stated over and over, these sources are simply not ready for prime time and won't be for years or even decades.

It is much more likely that oil and natural gas will be heavily relied upon to ensure that energy needs are met through 2040 and beyond, but this trend will not be impervious to price spikes and collapses. The market is an imperfect instrument for delivering goods and services (it just happens to be better than anything else). After a review of all the prevailing evidence and analysis, the prevailing view for oil, gas, and coal for the majority of this century is likely to be one of abundance, with periodic risks that demand can outstrip supply, as occurred in 2008. If history is a guide, such price spikes act as an economic incentive to increase exploration and extraction efforts, just as 2008 did, with the end result being a massive increase in supply to respond to the sharp price increase. As noted in prior chapters, this is Economics 101. As this chapter demonstrated early on, there are very sound reasons to believe the average daily rate of the production of crude oil in the United States will be at a minimum of roughly where it is now—9.2 million barrels per day for the next three decades. This nearly matches the 1970 peak, and oil as a percentage of GDP is much less today than it was then. Again this is an indicator of abundance, not scarcity. We will have all the oil and gas we need at for decades into the future at prices that are affordable, albeit often volatile, for the mass middle class.

Also bear in mind that projections for the share of renewables as a percentage of total energy generation is for them to rise from 21 percent in 2012 to 33 percent in 2040.[170] One needs to understand that this one-third share includes hydropower, an age-old source of energy dating back to the first time humans used the moving water in a creek to power a mill that ground wheat into flour. The share of wind, solar, biofuel, and geothermal energy will be much smaller. Additionally, by 2040, when renewables are expected to comprise one-third of all energy generation, it will require $205 billion in subsidies worldwide.[171] So while the expectation is for renewables to rapidly increase share of the total global energy mix over the next twenty-five years, it will require a constant and material investment of subsidies from the governments that promote their use. Take away the subsidies, and you either get a sharp reduction in the growth rate of renewables as a source of energy, or you stick with them and get skyrocketing costs. Neither is an optimal economical outcome.

---

170 Ibid.
171 Ibid.

The inescapable conclusion is that renewables will not replace fossil fuels until the latter part of the century (post-2050), and doing so will require continued massive subsidy of the renewable industry. Fossil fuels will be the workhorse for most of that period, as they have been for the past century. There is a very real possibility that renewables will become viable without needing government subsidy before we even reach the peak production of crude oil. Furthermore, given what we know now, peak oil is highly unlikely to occur before 2045 on a global basis and may well be delayed for decades beyond that. As noted earlier in this chapter, the United States will very likely produce at last 2.5 times present proved oil reserves over the next thirty years, and I calculated that to be roughly one hundred billion barrels of crude produced in the United States from now through 2045.

Also note that earlier in this chapter, I cited EIA data showing there are 220-plus billion barrels of technically recoverable crude oil in the United States (oil geologists know it is there, but it is not economically recoverable at today's prices, given today's technologies, or is off-limits as a matter of government policy). Assume I am correct in my predictions, and the United States produces the 100 billion barrels of oil domestically. I believe we will be left with 110 billion barrels of technically recoverable oil in the United States— in 2045! And trust me: if there is a sustained price spike— say $150-per-barrel oil comes and does not leave—then two things will happen: (1) federal prohibitions on drilling off-shore and other sacred locations will be eliminated quite quickly, and (2) there will also most certainly be additional discoveries of technically recoverable oil. Sustained $150-per-barrel oil and higher will be a massive incentive to find more of the stuff. Bet on it, and keep a skeptical eye on the peak-oil alarmists when you hear them, for they have a terrible track record.

I think it appropriate that the final word for this chapter and the book comes from the just-issued 2015 US Energy Information Administration (EIA) Annual Energy Outlook (hereafter AEO2015)—as always, a document that is loaded with pertinent information relating to energy matters. The most astonishing projection made in the AEO2015 is that "[t]hrough 2020, strong growth in domestic crude oil production from tight formations leads to a decline in net petroleum imports and growth in net petroleum product exports *in all AEO2015 Cases*" (emphasis added).[172] The Annual Energy Outlook publications by this agency are essentially projections in a number of different scenarios based on possibilities with prices and resource availability. What is noted here is that in all cases analyzed, the conclusion is that there is strong production growth expected in the extraction of crude oil in the United States—so much so that the reliance on imports continues to materially decline. Remember that ten years ago, the United States was importing nearly 60 percent of the crude oil it needed, and now, ten years later, it is

---

172 US Energy Information Administration, *2015 Annual Energy Outlook*, ES-1. Moreover, the agency flatly states that US crude oil from tight formations leads the growth in total US oil production in all AEO2015 cases. Ibid., E-4. Production is rising and will continue to rise for the rest of the decade as well as after that, albeit at a potentially slower rate.

exporting crude oil and natural gas for the first time in over half a century.

And the export business will have challenges of its own. Reuters recently reported that there were three thirty-seven-thousand-ton product tankers headed for Europe loaded with diesel fuel from the US Gulf Coast. They had to make a literal U-turn in the middle of the Atlantic Ocean because their destination ports were nearing full capacity to take on any more cargo.[173] Additionally, European prices of finished fuels (along with the price of crude) had collapsed, and European purchasers were unwilling to buy more at such low prices.[174] Even more astonishing are the new storage methods being employed by the US shale-gas industry. As the abundance of crude is so great and the price is under such pressure, companies are coming up with creative new ways to store the crude. One such way is to drill out the well but not complete the process, which is referred to as "drilled out but uncomplete," or DUC.[175] The thought being that the well would be easily tapped once prices rebound and would effectively be in underground storage until needed. By definition, this is much more a story of plenty than depravity, with the weight of information pointing in the direction of abundance as opposed to scarcity.

---

173 Reuters, *Product Tankers Turn Back as European Storage Fills,* December 19, 2015, www.maritime-executive.com/article/product-tankers-turn-back-as-european-storage-fills.

174 Ibid.

175 Clifford Krause, *Hoping for a Pricing Surge, Oil Companies Keep Wells in Reserve,* New York Times, December 26, 2015.

Another worthy note from AEO2015 is that the United States is to be a net exporter of natural gas by 2017—two years from the writing of this book, with the only real question being the amount of net exports. The country is expected to remain a net exporter through 2040—that is, the next quarter century.[176] A projection like this from an official government source (remember that the EIA is part of the Department of Energy, which is a cabinet-level position within the administration) would have been unimaginable a decade ago, which is yet another indicator of abundance being projected over the next twenty-five years. It may well be time to ask yourself if we are closer to the beginning of the fossil-fuel era than the end of it. For now, the only thing that is ending is the notion of petroleum scarcity. For the next few decades, anyway, peak oil be damned!

---

176 *See* note 171, *supra.*